TERRORISM RISK INSURANCE

ANALYSES AND PROSPECTS

ECONOMIC ISSUES, PROBLEMS AND PERSPECTIVES

Additional books in this series can be found on Nova's website
under the Series tab.

Additional E-books in this series can be found on Nova's website
under the E-book tab.

TERRORISM, HOT SPOTS AND CONFLICT-RELATED ISSUES

Additional books in this series can be found on Nova's website
under the Series tab.

Additional E-books in this series can be found on Nova's website
under the E-book tab.

ECONOMIC ISSUES, PROBLEMS AND PERSPECTIVES

TERRORISM RISK INSURANCE

ANALYSES AND PROSPECTS

OSCAR A. MADSEN
EDITOR

New York

For permission to use material from this book please contact us:
Telephone 631-231-7269; Fax 631-231-8175
Web Site: http://www.novapublishers.com

Additional color graphics may be available in the e-book version of this book.

Library of Congress Cataloging-in-Publication Data

ISBN: 978-1-62618-697-2

Published by Nova Science Publishers, Inc. † New York

CONTENTS

PREFACE

Prior to the September 11, 2011, terrorist attacks, insurance coverage for losses from such attacks was normally included in general insurance policies without specific cost to the policyholders. Following the attacks, such coverage became very expansive if insurers offered it at all. Because insurance is required for a variety of economic transactions, it was feared that the absence of insurance against terrorism loss would have a wider economic impact. Private terrorism insurance was largely unavailable for most of 2002 and some have argued that this adversely affected parts of the economy. Congress responded to the disruption in the terrorism insurance market by passing the Terrorism Risk Insurance Act of 2002 (TRIA). TRIA created a temporary three-year Terrorism Insurance Program in which the government would share some of the losses with private insurers should a foreign terrorist attack occur. This book analyzes the TRIA program at ten years and the future of the terrorism risk insurance program.

Chapter 1 - Prior to the September 11, 2001, terrorist attacks, insurance coverage for losses from such attacks was normally included in general insurance policies without specific cost to the policyholders. Following the attacks, such coverage became very expensive if insurers offered it at all. Because insurance is required for a variety of economic transactions, it was feared that the absence of insurance against terrorism loss would have a wider economic impact. Private terrorism insurance was largely unavailable for most of 2002 and some have argued that this adversely affected parts of the economy.

Congress responded to the disruption in the terrorism insurance market by passing the Terrorism Risk Insurance Act of 2002 (TRIA; P.L. 107-297, 116 Stat. 2322).

TRIA created a temporary three-year Terrorism Insurance Program in which the government would share some of the losses with private insurers should a foreign terrorist attack occur. This program was extended in 2005 (P.L. 109-144, 119 Stat. 2660) and 2007 (P.L. 110-160, 121 Stat. 1839). The amount of government loss sharing depends on the size of the insured loss. In general terms, for a relatively small loss, private industry covers the entire loss. For a medium-sized loss, the federal role is to spread the loss over time and over the entire insurance industry; the government assists insurers initially but then recoups the payments through a broad levy on insurers afterwards. For a large loss, the federal government would cover most of the losses, although recoupment is possible in these circumstances as well. Insurers are required to make terrorism coverage available to commercial policyholders, but TRIA does not require policyholders to purchase terrorism coverage. The prospective government share of losses has been reduced over time compared with the initial act, but the 2007 reauthorization expanded the program to cover losses stemming from acts of domestic terrorism. The TRIA program is currently slated to expire at the end of 2014.

The specifics of the current program are as follows: (1) a single terrorist act must cause $5 million in damage to be certified for TRIA coverage; (2) the aggregate insured loss from certified acts of terrorism must be $100 million in a year for the government coverage to begin; and (3) an individual company must meet a deductible of 20% of its annual premiums for the government coverage to begin. Once these thresholds are passed, the government covers 85% of insured losses due to terrorism. If aggregate insured losses due to terrorism do not exceed $27.5 billion, the Secretary of the Treasury is required to recoup 133% of the government coverage by the end of 2017 through surcharges on property/casualty insurance policies. If the losses exceed $27.5 billion, the Secretary has discretion to apply recoupment surcharges, but is not required to do so.

Since TRIA's passage, the private industry's willingness and ability to cover terrorism risk have increased. Prices for terrorism coverage have generally trended downward, and approximately 60% of commercial policyholders have purchased coverage over the past few years. This relative market calm has been under the umbrella of TRIA coverage, and it is unclear how the insurance market would react to the expiration of the federal program.

In the 113th Congress, Representative Michael Grimm has introduced H.R. 508 to extend the TRIA program's expiration date five years until the end of 2019. The bill has been referred to the House Committee on Financial Services, who has yet to take further action in this Congress. The committee's

Subcommittee on Insurance, Housing, and Community Opportunity held a hearing on TRIA during the 112th Congress.

Chapter 2 - This is the Testimony of Robert P. Hartwig, President, Insurance Information Institute. Hearing on "TRIA at Ten Years: The Future of the Terrorism Risk Insurance Program."

Chapter 3 - This is the Testimony of David C. John, Senior Research Fellow, The Heritage Foundation. Hearing on "TRIA at Ten Years: The Future of the Terrorism Risk Insurance Program."

Chapter 4 - This is the Statement of Rolf Lundberg, Senior Vice President, Co"TRIA at Ten Years: The Future of the Terrorism Risk Insurance Program."

Chapter 5 - This is the Testimony of Erwann O. Michel-Kerjan, Professor, Wharton School of Business, University of Pennslyvania. Hearing on "TRIA at Ten Years: The Future of the Terrorism Risk Insurance Program."

Chapter 6 - This is the Testimony of Janice Ochenkowski, Managing Director, Jones Lang LaSalle. Hearing on "TRIA at Ten Years: The Future of the Terrorism Risk Insurance Program."

Chapter 7 - This is the Testimony of Linda St. Peter, Operations Manager, Prudential Connecticut Realty. Hearing on "TRIA at Ten Years: The Future of the Terrorism Risk Insurance Program."

Chapter 8 - This is the Statement of Steve Bartlett, President and CEO, The Financial Services Roundtable. Hearing on "TRIA at Ten Years: The Future of the Terrorism Risk Insurance Program."

Chapter 9 - This is the Statement of Darwin Copeman, President and Chief Executive Officer, Jewelers Mutual Insurance Company. Hearing on "TRIA at Ten Years: The Future of the Terrorism Risk Insurance Program."

Chapter 10 - This is the Testimony of Michael Lanza, Executive Vice President and General Counsel, Selective Insurance Group, Inc. Hearing on "TRIA at Ten Years: The Future of the Terrorism Risk Insurance Program."

Chapter 11 - This is the Testimony of Christopher M. Lewis, Senior Vice President and Chief Insurance Risk Officer, The Hartford Financial Services Group. Hearing on "TRIA at Ten Years: The Future of the Terrorism Risk Insurance Program."

In: Terrorism Risk Insurance
Editor: Oscar A. Madsen

Chapter 1

TERRORISM RISK INSURANCE: ISSUE ANALYSIS AND OVERVIEW OF CURRENT PROGRAM[*]

Baird Webel

SUMMARY

Prior to the September 11, 2001, terrorist attacks, insurance coverage for losses from such attacks was normally included in general insurance policies without specific cost to the policyholders. Following the attacks, such coverage became very expensive if insurers offered it at all. Because insurance is required for a variety of economic transactions, it was feared that the absence of insurance against terrorism loss would have a wider economic impact. Private terrorism insurance was largely unavailable for most of 2002 and some have argued that this adversely affected parts of the economy.

Congress responded to the disruption in the terrorism insurance market by passing the Terrorism Risk Insurance Act of 2002 (TRIA; P.L. 107-297, 116 Stat. 2322).

TRIA created a temporary three-year Terrorism Insurance Program in which the government would share some of the losses with private insurers should a foreign terrorist attack occur. This program was

---

[*] This is an edited, reformatted and augmented version of a Congressional Research Service publication, CRS Report for Congress R42716, from www.crs.gov, prepared for Members and Committees of Congress, dated February 26, 2013.

extended in 2005 (P.L. 109-144, 119 Stat. 2660) and 2007 (P.L. 110-160, 121 Stat. 1839). The amount of government loss sharing depends on the size of the insured loss. In general terms, for a relatively small loss, private industry covers the entire loss. For a medium-sized loss, the federal role is to spread the loss over time and over the entire insurance industry; the government assists insurers initially but then recoups the payments through a broad levy on insurers afterwards. For a large loss, the federal government would cover most of the losses, although recoupment is possible in these circumstances as well. Insurers are required to make terrorism coverage available to commercial policyholders, but TRIA does not require policyholders to purchase terrorism coverage. The prospective government share of losses has been reduced over time compared with the initial act, but the 2007 reauthorization expanded the program to cover losses stemming from acts of domestic terrorism. The TRIA program is currently slated to expire at the end of 2014.

The specifics of the current program are as follows: (1) a single terrorist act must cause $5 million in damage to be certified for TRIA coverage; (2) the aggregate insured loss from certified acts of terrorism must be $100 million in a year for the government coverage to begin; and (3) an individual company must meet a deductible of 20% of its annual premiums for the government coverage to begin. Once these thresholds are passed, the government covers 85% of insured losses due to terrorism. If aggregate insured losses due to terrorism do not exceed $27.5 billion, the Secretary of the Treasury is required to recoup 133% of the government coverage by the end of 2017 through surcharges on property/casualty insurance policies. If the losses exceed $27.5 billion, the Secretary has discretion to apply recoupment surcharges, but is not required to do so.

Since TRIA's passage, the private industry's willingness and ability to cover terrorism risk have increased. Prices for terrorism coverage have generally trended downward, and approximately 60% of commercial policyholders have purchased coverage over the past few years. This relative market calm has been under the umbrella of TRIA coverage, and it is unclear how the insurance market would react to the expiration of the federal program.

In the 113th Congress, Representative Michael Grimm has introduced H.R. 508 to extend the TRIA program's expiration date five years until the end of 2019. The bill has been referred to the House Committee on Financial Services, who has yet to take further action in this Congress. The committee's Subcommittee on Insurance, Housing, and Community Opportunity held a hearing on TRIA during the 112th Congress.

INTRODUCTION

Prior to the September 2001, terrorist attacks on the United States, insurers generally did not exclude or separately charge for coverage of terrorism risks. The events of September 11, 2001, changed this as insurers realized the extent of possible terrorism losses. Estimates of insured losses from the 9/11 attacks are around $40 billion in current dollars, the largest insured losses from a non-natural disaster on record. These losses were concentrated in business interruption insurance (33% of the losses), property insurance (30%), and liability insurance (23%).[1]

Although primary insurance companies, those who actually sell and service the insurance policies bought by consumers, suffered losses from the terrorist attacks, the heaviest insured losses were absorbed by foreign and domestic reinsurers—the insurers of insurance companies. Because of the lack of public data on, or modeling of, the scope and nature of the terrorism risk, reinsurers felt unable to accurately price for such risks and largely withdrew from the market for terrorism risk insurance in the months following September 11, 2001. Once reinsurers stopped offering coverage for terrorism risk, primary insurers, suffering equally from a lack of public data and models, also withdrew, or tried to withdraw, from the market. In most states, state regulators must approve policy form changes. Most state regulators agreed to insurer requests to exclude terrorism risks from commercial policies, just as these policies had long excluded war risks. Terrorism risk insurance was soon unavailable or extremely expensive, and many businesses were no longer able to purchase insurance that would protect them in future terrorist attacks. Although the evidence is largely anecdotal, some were concerned that the lack of coverage posed a threat of serious harm to the real estate, transportation, construction, energy, and utility sectors, in turn threatening the broader economy.

In November 2002, Congress responded to the fears of economic damage due to the absence of commercially available coverage for terrorism with passage of the Terrorism Risk Insurance Act[2] (TRIA). TRIA created a three-year Terrorism Risk Insurance Program to provide a government reinsurance backstop in the case of terrorist attack. The TRIA program was amended and extended in 2005[3] and 2007.[4] Following the 2007 amendments, the TRIA program is set to expire at the end of 2014. (A side-by-side of the original law and the two reauthorization acts can be found below in *Table 1*.)

Although the expiration date is not until the end of the 113th Congress, the 112th Congress took notice of the issue. Senator Roger Wicker filed an amendment to change the expiration date of TRIA from 2014 to 2013 during a Senate markup, although he ultimately did not offer this amendment. The House Financial Services Subcommittee on Insurance, Housing, and Community Opportunity held a hearing on September 11, 2012, entitled "TRIA at Ten Years: The Future of the Terrorism Risk Insurance Program."[5]

The executive branch has been skeptical about the TRIA program in the past. Bills to expand TRIA were resisted by then-President George W. Bush's Administration,[6] and previous presidential budgets under President Obama called for changes in the program that would have had the effect of scaling back the coverage for terrorist attacks. Congress declined to act on these budgetary proposals at the time and no such legislative proposals were contained in the President's FY2013 budget proposal. The insurance industry largely continues to support TRIA,[7] as do the real estate and other industries who have formed a "Coalition to Insure Against Terrorism"(CIAT).[8]

THE TERRORISM RISK INSURANCE ACT OF 2002 REAUTHORIZATION ACT OF 2013 (H.R. 508)

Representative Michael Grimm along with 9 cosponsors introduced H.R. 508 on February 5, 2013. The bill is a reauthorization of the existing TRIA program that would extend the program five years until the end of 2019. It would also extend the time period for mandatory recoupment seven years until September 30, 2024. The bill has been referred to the House Committee on Financial Services.

Specifics of the Current TRIA Program

The original TRIA legislation's stated goals were to (1) create a temporary federal program of shared public and private compensation for insured terrorism losses to allow the private market to stabilize; (2) protect consumers by ensuring the availability and affordability of insurance for terrorism risks; and (3) preserve state regulation of insurance. Although Congress has amended specific aspects of the original act, the general operation of the program largely follows the original statute. The changes to the program have largely reduced the government coverage for terrorism losses, except that the

2007 amendments expanded coverage to losses due to domestic terrorism, rather than limiting the program to foreign terrorism.

To meet the *first* goal, the TRIA program creates a mechanism through which the federal government could share insured commercial property/casualty[9] losses with the private insurance market. The role of federal loss sharing depends on the size of the insured loss. For a relatively small loss, there is no federal sharing. For a medium-sized loss, the federal role is to spread the loss over time and over the entire insurance industry, providing assistance up front but then recouping the payments through a broad levy on insurance policies afterwards. For a large loss, the federal government is to pay most of the losses, although recoupment is possible in these circumstances as well.

The precise criteria under the current TRIA program are as follows:

1. An individual act of terrorism must be certified jointly by the Secretary of the Treasury, Secretary of State, and Attorney General; losses must exceed $5 million in the United States or to U.S. air carriers or sea vessels for an act of terrorism to be certified.

2. The federal government shares in an insurer's losses only if the insurance industry's aggregate insured losses from certified acts of terrorism exceed $100 million.

3. The federal program covers only commercial property and casualty insurance, and excludes by statute several specific lines of insurance.[10]

4. Each insurer is responsible for paying out a certain amount in claims—known as its deductible—before receiving federal coverage. An insurer's deductible is proportionate to its size, equaling 20% of an insurer's annual direct earned premiums the commercial property/casualty lines of insurance specified in TRIA.

5. Once the $100 million aggregate loss threshold and 20% deductible are passed, the federal government is to cover 85% of each insurer's losses above its deductible until the amount of losses totals $100 billion.

6. After $100 billion in aggregate losses, there is no federal government coverage and no requirement that insurers provide coverage.

7. In the years following the federal sharing of insurer losses, but prior to September 30, 2017, the Secretary of the Treasury is required to establish surcharges on property/casualty insurers to recoup 133% of the outlays to insurers under the program. This mandatory recoupment

will not apply, if the insurance industry's aggregate uncompensated loss exceeds $27.5 billion; in this case, however, the Treasury Secretary retains discretionary authority to apply recoupment surcharges.

The initial loss sharing under TRIA can be seen in *Figure 1* below, adapted from a report by the Congressional Budget Office (CBO). The exact amount of the 20% deductible at which TRIA coverage would begin depends on how the losses are distributed among insurance companies. In the aggregate, 20% of the direct-earned premiums for all of the property/casualty lines specified in TRIA totaled approximately $34 billion according to 2011 data supplied by the National Association of Insurance Commissioners (NAIC). TRIA coverage is likely, however, to begin under this amount as the losses from an attack are unlikely to be equally distributed among insurance companies.

TRIA addresses the *second* goal, to protect consumers, by requiring those insurers that offer the lines of insurance covered by TRIA to make terrorism insurance available prospectively to their commercial policyholders. This coverage may not differ materially from coverage for other types of losses. Each terrorism insurance offer must reveal both the premium charged for terrorism insurance and the possible federal share of compensation. Policyholders are not, however, required to purchase coverage. If the policyholder declines to purchase terrorism coverage, its insurer can exclude terrorism losses. The law itself does not limit what insurers can charge for terrorism risk insurance, though state regulators typically have the authority under state law to modify excessive, inadequate, or unfairly discriminatory rates.

TRIA's *third* goal, to preserve state regulation of insurance, is expressly accomplished in Section 106(a), which provides "Nothing in this title shall affect the jurisdiction or regulatory authority of the insurance commissioner [of a state]." The Section 106(a) provision has two exceptions: (1) the federal statute preempts any state definition of an "act of terrorism" in favor of the federal definition and (2) state rate and form approval laws for terrorism insurance were preempted from enactment to the end of 2003. In addition to these exceptions, Section 105 of the law also preempts state laws with respect to insurance policy exclusions for acts of terrorism.

The administration of the TRIA program was originally left generally to the Secretary of the Treasury. This was changed somewhat in the Dodd-Frank Wall Street Reform and Consumer Protection Act of 2010.[11]

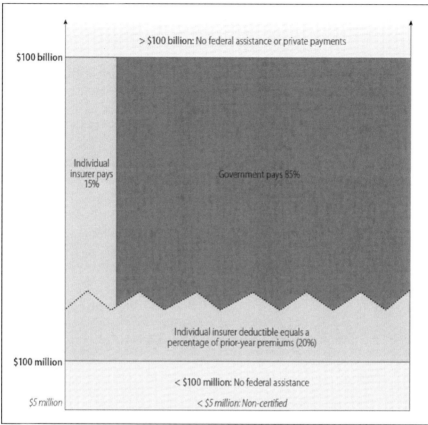

Source: Congressional Research Service, adapted from Congressional Budget Office,
Federal Reinsurance for Terrorism Risks: Issues in Reauthorization, August, 2007,
p. 12.

Note: Aggregate of all individual insurer deductibles totaled approximately $34 billion
in 2011, according to the NAIC.

Figure 1. Initial Loss Sharing Under Current TRIA Program.

This act created a new Federal Insurance Office (FIO) to be located in the
Department of the Treasury. Among the duties specified for the FIO in the
legislation was to assist the Secretary in the administration of the Terrorism
Insurance Program.[12]

No acts of terrorism meeting the requirements for coverage under the
program have occurred since the passage of TRIA.

COVERAGE FOR NUCLEAR, CHEMICAL, BIOLOGICAL, AND RADIOLOGICAL TERRORISM

A terrorist attack with some form of nuclear, chemical, biological, or radiological (NCBR)[13] weapon would often be considered the most likely type of attack causing large scale losses. The current TRIA statute does not specifically include or exclude NCBR events; thus, the TRIA program in general would cover insured losses from terrorist actions due to NCBR as it would for an attack by conventional means. The term *insured losses*, however, is a meaningful distinction. Most insurance policies that would fall under the TRIA umbrella include exclusions that would likely limit insurer coverage of an NCBR event, whether it was due to terrorism or to some sort of accident, although these exclusions have never been legally tested in the United States after a terrorist event.[14] If these exclusions are invoked and do indeed limit the insurer losses due to NCBR terrorism, they would also limit the TRIA coverage of such losses. Language that would have specifically extended TRIA coverage to NCBR events was offered in the past,[15] but was not included in legislation as enacted. In 2007, the Government Accountability Office (GAO) was directed to study the issue and a GAO report was issued in 2008.[16]

BACKGROUND ON TERRORISM INSURANCE

Insurability of Terrorism Risk

Stripped to its most basic elements, insurance is a fairly straightforward operation. An insurer agrees to assume an indefinite future risk in exchange for a definite current premium from a consumer. The insurer pools a large number of risks such that at any given point in time, the ongoing losses will not be larger than the current premiums being paid, plus the residual amount of past premiums that the insurer retains and invests, plus, in a last resort, any borrowing against future profits if this is possible. For the insurer to operate successfully and avoid bankruptcy, it is critical to accurately estimate the probability of a loss and the severity of that loss so that a sufficient premium can be charged. Insurers generally depend upon huge databases of past loss information in setting these rates. Everyday occurrences, such as automobile accidents or natural deaths, can be estimated with great accuracy.

Extraordinary events, such as large hurricanes, are more difficult, but insurers have many years of weather data, coupled with sophisticated computer models, with which to make predictions.

Terrorism risk is seen by many to be so fundamentally different from other risks as to be essentially uninsurable by the private insurance market, and thus requiring a government solution. The argument that terrorism risk is uninsurable typically focuses on lack of public data about both the probability and severity of terrorist acts. The reason for the lack of historical data would generally be seen as a good thing—very few terrorist attacks are attempted and fewer have succeeded. This, however, does not assuage the fiduciary duty of an insurance company president not to put a company at risk by insuring against an event that could bankrupt the firm. As a replacement for large amounts of historical data, insurers turn to various forms of models similar to those used to assess future hurricane losses. Even the best model, however, can only partly replace good data, and terrorism models are still relatively new compared with hurricane models.

One prominent insurance textbook identifies four ideal elements of an insurable risk: (1) a sufficiently large number of insureds to make losses reasonably predictable; (2) losses must be definite and measurable; (3) losses must be fortuitous or accidental; and (4) losses must not be catastrophic (i.e., it must be unlikely to produce losses to a large percentage of the risks at the same time).[17] Terrorism risk in the United States would appear to fail the first criterion. It also likely fails the third due to the malevolent human actors behind terrorist attacks, whose motives, means, and targets of attack are constantly in flux. Whether it fails the fourth criterion is largely decided by the underwriting actions of insurers themselves (i.e., whether the insurers insure a large number of risks in a single geographic area that would be affected by a terrorist strike). Unsurprisingly, insurers generally have sought to limit their exposures in particular geographic locations with a conceptually higher risk for terrorist attacks, making terrorism insurance more difficult to find in those areas.

International Experience with Terrorism Risk Insurance

Although the U.S. experience with terrorism is relatively limited, other countries have dealt with the issue more extensively and have developed their own responses to the challenges presented by terrorism risk. Spain, which has seen significant terrorist activity by Basque separatist movements, insures against acts of terrorism via a broader government-owned reinsurer that has provided coverage for catastrophes since 1954.

The United Kingdom, responding the Irish Republican Army attacks in the 1980s, created Pool Re, a privately owned mutual insurance company with government backing, specifically to insure terrorism risk. In the aftermath of the September 11, 2001, attacks, many foreign countries reassessed their terrorism risk and created a variety of approaches to deal with the risk. The UK greatly expanded Pool Re, whereas Germany created a private insurer with government backing to offer terrorism insurance policies. Germany's plan, like TRIA in the United States, was created as a temporary measure. It has been extended since its inception and it is now set to expire at the end of 2013.[18]

Not all countries, however, concluded that some sort of government backing for terrorism insurance was necessary. Canada specifically considered, and rejected, creating a government program following September 11, 2001.

Previous U.S. Experience with "Uninsurable" Risks

Terrorism risk post-2001 is not the first time the United States has faced a risk perceived as uninsurable in private markets that Congress chooses to address through government action.

During World War II, for example, Congress created a "war damage" insurance program, and there are current programs insuring against aviation war risk[19] and flood losses,[20] respectively.

The closest previous analog to the situation with terrorism risk may be the federal riot reinsurance program created in the late 1960s. Following large scale riots in American cities in the late 1960s, insurers generally pulled back from insuring in those markets, either adding policy exclusions to limit their exposure to damage from riots or ceasing to sell property damage insurance altogether. In response, Congress created a riot reinsurance program as part of the Housing and Urban Development Act of 1968.[21] The federal riot reinsurance program offered reinsurance contracts similar to commercial excess reinsurance. The government agreed to cover some percentage of an insurance company's losses above a certain deductible in exchange for a premium paid by that insurance company. Private reinsurers eventually returned to the market and the federal riot reinsurance program was terminated in 1985.

THE TERRORISM INSURANCE MARKET

Post-9/11 and Pre-TRIA

The September 2001 terrorist attacks, and the resulting billions of dollars in insured losses, caused significant upheaval in the insurance market. Even before the attacks, the insurance market was showing signs of a cyclical "hardening" of the market in which prices typically rise and availability is somewhat limited. The unexpectedly large losses caused by terrorist acts exacerbated this trend, especially with respect to the commercial lines of insurance most at risk for terrorism losses. Post-September 11, insurers and reinsurers started including substantial surcharges for terrorism risk, or, more commonly, they excluded coverage for terrorist attacks altogether. Reinsurers could take these steps rapidly because reinsurance contracts and rates are generally unregulated. Primary insurance contracts and rates are more closely regulated by the individual states and the exclusion of terrorism coverage for the individual purchaser of insurance required regulatory approval at the state level in most cases. States acted fairly quickly, and, by early 2002, 45 states had approved insurance policy language prepared by the Insurance Services Office, Inc. (ISO, an insurance consulting firm), excluding terrorism damage in standard commercial policies.[22]

The lack of readily available terrorism insurance caused fears of a larger economic impact, particularly on the real estate market. In most cases, lenders prefer or require that a borrower maintain insurance coverage on a property. Lack of terrorism insurance coverage could lead to defaults on existing loans and a downturn in future lending, causing economic ripple effects as buildings are not built and construction workers remain idle. The 14-month period after the September 2001 terrorist attacks and before the November 2002 passage of TRIA provides some insight into the effects of a lack of terrorism insurance. Some examples in September 2002 include the Real Estate Round Table releasing a survey finding that "$15.5 billion of real estate projects in 17 states were stalled or cancelled because of a continuing scarcity of terrorism insurance"[23] and Moody's Investors Service downgrading $4.5 billion in commercial mortgage-backed securities.[24] This picture, however, was not uniform. For example, in July 2002, the *Wall Street Journal* reported that "despite concerns over landlords' ability to get terrorism insurance, trophy properties were in demand."[25] Aside from such anecdotes, there is little hard data to form judgments about what effect the lack of terrorism coverage had on the economy in this time period.

After TRIA

The "make available" provisions of TRIA addressed the availability problem in the terrorism insurance market, as insurers were required by law to offer commercial terrorism coverage.

There was significant uncertainty, however, as to how businesses would react, because there was no general requirement to purchase terrorism coverage[26] and the pricing of terrorism coverage was initially high. Initial consumer reaction to the terrorism coverage offers was relatively subdued. Marsh, Inc., a large insurance broker, reports that only 27% of their clients bought terrorism insurance in 2003.

This take-up rate, however, climbed relatively quickly to 49% in 2004 and 58% in 2005. Since 2005, the take-up rate has stayed near 60%, with Marsh reporting 65% in 2011.[27]

The price for terrorism insurance has appeared to decline over the past decade, although available pricing data is based on surveys; thus, the level of pricing may not always be comparable between sources. The 2006 and 2010 reports by the President's Working Group on Financial Markets show a high of above 7% for the median terrorism premium as a percentage of the total property premium in 2003, with a generally downward trend, and the latest values between 3% and 4%.[28]

These values were reported by Aon, another major insurance broker. While the trend may be downward, there has been significant variability, with a rate above 6% reported in the 4th quarter of 2006. There is also significant variability across industries. For example, Marsh reported rates in 2009 as high as 24% of the property premium for financial institutions and as low as 2% in the food and beverage industry.[29]

The willingness of insurers to cover terrorism risk, as well as their financial capability to do so, has increased over the past decade. From the late 2001 and 2002 marketplace, where terrorism coverage was essentially unavailable, the latest estimates from the insurance broker Guy Carpenter are that between $6 billion and $8 billion in terrorism reinsurance capacity is available in the U.S. market. The combined policyholder surplus among all U.S. property/casualty insurers was $551.8 billion at the start of 2012, up from $293.5 billion at the start of 2002.[30] This amount, however, backs all policies in the United States and is subject to depletion in a wide variety of events. Extreme weather losses could particularly draw capital away from the terrorism insurance market, as such weather events share some risk characteristics with large terrorist attacks.

EVOLUTION OF TERRORISM RISK INSURANCE LAWS

Table 1 presents a side-by-side comparison of the original TRIA law, along with the reauthorizing laws from 2005 and 2007.

Table 1. Side-by-Side of Terrorism Risk Insurance Laws

Provision	15 U.S.C. 6701 Note (P.L. 107-297)	P.L. 109-144	P.L. 110-160
Title	Terrorism Risk Insurance Act of 2002	Terrorism Risk Insurance Extension Act of 2005	Terrorism Risk Insurance Program Reauthorization Act of 2007
Expiration Date	December 31, 2005 (Sec. 108(a))	December 31, 2007 (Sec. 2)	December 31, 2014 (Sec. 3(a))
"Act of Terrorism" Definition	For an act of terrorism to be covered under TRIA, it must be a violent act committed on behalf of a foreign person or interest as part of an effort to coerce the U.S. civilian population or influence U.S. government policy. It must have resulted in damage within the United States or to a U.S. airliner or mission abroad. Terrorist act is to be certified by the Secretary of the Treasury in concurrence with the Attorney General and Secretary of State. (Sec. 102(1)(A))	No Change	Removed requirement that a covered act of terrorism be committed on behalf of a foreign person or interest. (Sec. 2)

Table 1. (Continued)

Limitation on Act of Terrorism Certification in Case of War	Terrorist act would not be covered in the event of a war, except for workers compensation insurance. (Sec. 102(1)(B)(I))	No Change	No Change
Minimum Damage To Be Certified	Terrorist act must cause more than $5 million in property and casualty insurance losses to be covered. (Sec. 102(1)(B)(ii))	No Change	No Change
Aggregate Industry Loss Requirement/Program Trigger	No Provision	Created a "program trigger" that would prevent coverage under the program unless aggregate industry losses exceed $50 million in 2006 and $100 million for 2007. (Sec. 6)	No Change. Program trigger remains at $100 million until 2014. (Sec. 3 (c))
Insurer Deductible	7% of earned premium for 2003, 10% of earned premium for 2004, 15% of earned premium for 2005. (Sec. 102(7))	Raised deductible to 17.5% for 2006 and 20% for 2007. (Sec. 3)	No Change. Deductible remains at 20% until 2014. (Sec. 3(c))
Covered Lines of Insurance	Commercial property/ casualty insurance, including excess insurance, workers' compensation, and surety but excluding crop insurance, private mortgage insurance, title	Excluded commercial auto, burglary and theft, professional liability (except for directors and officers liability), and farm owners multiple peril from coverage. (Sec. 3)	No change from P.L. 109-144

	insurance, financial guaranty insurance, medical malpractice insurance, health or life insurance, flood insurance, or reinsurance. (Sec. 102(12))		
Mandatory Availability	Every insurer must make terrorism coverage that does not differ materially from coverage applicable to losses other than terrorism. (Sec. 103(c))	No Change. Mandatory availability extended through 2007. (Sec. 2(b))	No Change. Mandatory availability extended through 2014. (Sec. 3(c))
Insured Shared Loss Compensation	Federal share of losses willbe 90% for insured losses that exceed the applicable insurer deductible. (Sec. 103(e))	Reduced federal share of losses to 85% for 2007. (Sec. 4)	No Change. Federal share remains at 85% through 2014.
Cap on Annual Liability	Federal share of compensation paid under the program will not exceed $100 million and insurers are not liable for any portion of losses that exceed $100 million unless Congress acts otherwise to cover these losses. (Sec. 103(e))	No Change	Removed the possibility that a future Congress could require insurers to cover some share of losses above $100,000,000,000 if the insurer has met its individual deductible. Requires insurers to clearly disclose this to policy holders. (Sec. 4(a) and Sec. 4(d))
Payment Procedures if Losses Exceed $100,000,000,000	After notice by the Secretary of the Treasury, Congress determines the procedures for payments if losses	No Change	Required Secretary of the Treasury to publish regulations within 240 days of passage regarding payments if losses exceed $100 billion. (Sec. 4(c))

Table 1. (Continued)

Payment Procedures if Losses Exceed $100,000,000,000	exceed $100 billion. (Sec. 103(e)(3))		
Aggregate Retention Amount Maximum	$10 billion for 2002-2003, $12.5 billion for 2004, $15 billion for 2005 (Sec. 103(6))	Raises amount to $25 billion for 2006 and $27.5 billion for 2007. (Sec. 5)	No Change. Aggregate retention remains at $27.5 billion through 2014.
Mandatory Recoupment of Federal Share	If insurer losses are under the aggregate retention amount, a mandatory recoupment of the federal share of the loss will be imposed. If insurer losses are over the aggregate retention amount, such recoupment is at the discretion of the Secretary of the Treasury. (Sec. 103(e)(7))	No Change	Increases total recoupment amount to be collected by the premium surcharges to 133% of the previously defined mandatory recoupment amount.(Sec. 4(e)(1)(A))
Recoupment Surcharge	Surcharge is limited to 3% of property-casualty insurance premium and may be adjusted by the Secretary to take into account the economic impact of the surcharge on urban commercial centers, the differential risk factors related to rural areas and smaller commercial centers, and the various exposures to terrorism risk	No Change	Removes 3% limit for mandatory surcharge. (Sec. 4(e)(2)(A))

	across lines of insurance. (Sec. 103(8))		

Source: Congressional Research Service, using Public Laws obtained from the Government Printing Office through http://www.congress.gov.

Notes: Section numbers for the initial TRIA law are as codified in 15 U.S.C 6701 note. Section numbers for P.L. 109-144 and P.L. 110-160 are from the legislation as enacted.

End Notes

[1] Robert P. Hartwig and Claire Wilkinson, "Terrorism Risk: A Reemergent Threat," April 2011, available on the Insurance Information Institute website at http://www.insureagain stterrorism.org/TerrorismRiskRe emergentThreat.pdf.

[2] P.L. 107-297, 116 Stat. 2322, codified at 15 U.S.C. 6701 note. For more information, see CRS Report RS21444, The Terrorism Risk Insurance Act of 2002: A Summary of Provisions, by Baird Webel.

[3] P.L. 109-144, 119 Stat. 2660. For more information, see CRS Report RL33177, Terrorism Risk Insurance Legislation in 2005: Issue Summary and Side-by-Side, by Baird Webel.

[4] P.L. 110-160, 121 Stat 1839. For more information, see CRS Report RL34219, Terrorism Risk Insurance Legislation in 2007: Issue Summary and Side-by-Side, by Baird Webel.

[5] U.S. Congress, House Committee on Financial Services, Subcommittee on Insurance, Housing and Community Opportunity, TRIA at Ten Years: The Future of the Terrorism Risk Insurance Program, 112th Cong., 2nd sess., September 11, 2012. Hearing testimony can be found at http://financialservices.house.gov/calendar/eventsingle.aspx? EventID=307443.

[6] See, for example, the Statement of Administration Policy on H.R. 2761 dated December 11, 2007, available at http://www.whitehouse.gov/sites/ default/files/omb/legislative/sap/110-1/hr2761sap-h.pdf.

[7] See, for example, American Insurance Association, "Aia Statement On Introduction Of TRIA Legislation," press release, February 5, 2013, http://www.aiadc.org/aiadotnet/ docHandler.aspx?DocID=355930.

[8] See the CIAT website at http://www.insureagainstterrorism.org.

[9] Commercial insurance is generally that insurance purchased by businesses in contrast to personal lines of insurance, which is purchased by individuals. This means that damage to individual homes and autos would not be covered under the TRIA program. Property/casualty insurance includes most lines of insurance except for life insurance and health insurance.

[10] Named lines of insurance that are not covered are federal crop insurance, private crop or livestock insurance, private mortgage insurance, title insurance, financial guaranty insurance of single-line guaranty insurers, medical malpractice, flood insurance, reinsurance, and all life insurance products.

[11] P.L. 111-203, 124 Stat. 1376.

[12] Section 502 of P.L. 111-203, codified at 31 U.S.C. 313(c)(1)(D).

[13] There is some variance in the acronym used for such attacks. The U.S. Department of Defense, for example, uses "CBRN," rather than NCBR, in its Dictionary of Military and Associated Terms; see p. 86 at http://www.scribd.com/ doc/25603718/The-DOD-Lexicon-JP1-02.

[14] It should be noted that insurers might have attempted to exclude the September 11, 2001, losses under existing war risk exclusions, but did not generally attempt to do so.

[15] See, for example, H.R. 2761 (110th Congress) as passed by the House on September 19, 2007, and H.Rept. 110-318, available at http://www.gpo.gov/fdsys/pkg/CRPT-110hrpt318/pdf/ CRPT-110hrpt318.pdf.

[16] U.S. Government Accountability Office, TERRORISM INSURANCE: Status of Coverage Availability for Attacks Involving Nuclear, Biological, Chemical, or Radiological Weapons, GAO-09-39, December 12, 2008, at http://gao.gov/ products/GAO-09-39.

[17] Emmett J. Vaughan and Therese Vaughan, Fundamentals of Risk and Insurance (Hoboken, NJ: John Wiley & Sons, 2003), p. 41.

[18] More information on foreign countries' programs can be found in pages 8-11 of the testimony of Erwann O. MichelKerjan at the previously mentioned September 11, 2012, House Financial Subcommittee hearing available at http://financialservices.house.gov/ uploadedfiles/hhrg-112-ba04-wstate-emichelkerjan-20120911.pdf.

[19] For more information, see http://www.faa.gov/about/office_org/headquarters_offices/ apl/aviation_insurance/.

[20] For more information, see CRS Report R40650, National Flood Insurance Program: Background, Challenges, and Financial Status, by Rawle O. King.

[21] P.L. 90-448, 82 Stat. 476. The act also created state "Fair Access to Insurance Requirements" (FAIR) plans and a Federal Crime Insurance Program.

[22] Jeff Woodward, "The ISO Terrorism Exclusions: Background and Analysis," IRMI Insights, February 2002, available at http://www.irmi.com/expert/articles/2002/woodward02.aspx.

[23] "Terror Insurance Drag on Real Estate Still Climbing," Real Estate Roundtable, September 19, 2003, available at http://www.rer.org/media/newsreleases/TRIA_Survey _15billion_ Sept19_2002.cfm.

[24] "Moody's Downgrades Securities on Lack of Terrorism Insurance," Wall Street Journal, September 30, 2002, p. C14.

[25] "Office-Building Demand Rises Despite Vacancies," Wall Street Journal, July 24, 2002, p. B6.

[26] Although there is no requirement in federal law to purchase terrorism coverage, businesses may be required by state law to purchase the coverage. This is particularly the case in workers compensation insurance. Market forces, such as requirements for commercial loans, may also compel purchase of terrorism coverage.

[27] Marsh, Inc., The Marsh Report Terrorism Risk Insurance 2010, p. 10, and U.S. Insurance Market Report 2012, Property, available at http://usa.marsh.com/NewsInsights/ GlobalIMR/IMRContent/ID/19468/US-Insurance-MarketReport-2012-Property.aspx.

[28] President's Working Group on Financial Markets, Terrorism Risk Insurance, September 2006, p. 37, and Market Conditions for Terrorism Risk Insurance, 2010, p. 30.

[29] Marsh, Inc., The Marsh Report Terrorism Risk Insurance 2010, p. 14.

[30] AM Best, Best's Aggregates & Averages, Property-Casualty, 2002 Edition, p. 2 and AM Best Statistical Study, "U.S. Property/Casualty—2011 Financial Results," March 26, 2012, p. 1.

In: Terrorism Risk Insurance
Editor: Oscar A. Madsen

ISBN: 978-1-62618-697-2
© 2013 Nova Science Publishers, Inc.

Chapter 2

TESTIMONY OF ROBERT P. HARTWIG, PRESIDENT, INSURANCE INFORMATION INSTITUTE. HEARING ON "TRIA AT TEN YEARS: THE FUTURE OF THE TERRORISM RISK INSURANCE PROGRAM"[*]

Thank you, Representative Biggert, Ranking Member Gutierrez and members of the Committee.

Good morning. My name is Robert Hartwig and I am President and Economist for the Insurance Information Institute, an international property/casualty insurance trade association based in New York City.[1] I am also a Chartered Property Casualty Underwriter (CPCU) and have worked on a wide variety of insurance issues during my 19 years in the property/casualty insurance and reinsurance industries, including many related to the industry's exposure to catastrophic loss, including acts or terrorism. The Institute's members account for nearly 70 percent of all property/casualty insurance premiums written in the United States. Its primary mission is to improve understanding of the insurance industry and the key role it plays in the global economy.

I have been asked by the Committee to provide testimony on the status of the market for terrorism insurance in the United States. For the purposes of my testimony, I will divide my testimony into the following major sections:

---

[*] This is an edited, reformatted and augmented version of a testimony presented September 11, 2012 before the House Committee on Financial Services, Subcommittee on Insurance, Housing and Community Opportunity.

1. Review of the impacts of the September 11, 2001 attacks on the insurance industry;
2. A brief summary of changes in the terrorism threat landscape since the enact of the original TRIA legislation in 2002;
3. A discussion of why most terrorism risk remains fundamentally uninsurable in the private insurance and reinsurance markets;
4. The impact of the Terrorism Risk Insurance Program in maintaining market stability;
5. Obstacles to insuring and reinsuring losses arising from acts of terrorism;
6. The success of the Terrorism Risk Insurance Program and the current state of the market for terrorism coverage, and;
7. Possible options for expanding private sector terrorism coverage.

SUMMARY OF IMPACTS ON THE SEPTEMBER 11, 2001 TERRORIST ATTACK ON INSURERS AND INSURANCE MARKETS

The terrorist attacks of September 11, 2001, produced insured losses larger than any natural or man-made event in history. Claims paid by insurers to their policyholders eventually totaled some $32.5 billion dollars--$40.0 billion in 2011 dollars (*Exhibit 1*) and to this day remain the second most costly insurance event in United States history (*Exhibit 2*).[2] The losses sustained by the insurance industry that fateful day were unprecedented in virtually every respect, producing catastrophic losses not only in property coverages, but also for the first time in life insurance, disability and workers compensation lines.

Aviation insurers also suffered their worst-ever losses stemming from a single event.

The sheer enormity of the loss—coming from an entirely unforeseen peril for which no premium had been collected—combined with the possibility of future attacks and uncertainty arising from the United States' rapid military response to the threat, produced financial shockwaves that shook insurance markets worldwide and provoked an extraordinarily swift and severe underwriting and pricing reaction by insurers and reinsurers.

Terrorism Exclusions and Price Shocks in the Wake of the 9/11 Attack

The shock of the September 11 attack led insurers and reinsurers to exclude coverage arising from acts of terrorism from virtually all commercial property and liability policies. Before 9/11 terrorism exclusions were virtually nonexistent in commercial insurance contracts sold in the United States. The economic consequences of such exclusions were quick to manifest themselves. Major commercial property construction projects around the country, unable to secure coverage against the now very real risk of terrorist attack, were in jeopardy of being tabled, hurting job growth at a time of rapidly rising unemployment and when much of the country was in recession. Banks, in turn, threatened to choke off lending to businesses if borrowers failed to secure coverage against terrorist acts. The problem was not confined to high profile "trophy" properties located in major metropolitan areas. Shopping malls, office complexes, factories, sports stadiums, hotels, utilities, airports, port facilities and other critical infrastructure all across the United States were impacted.

Even as exclusions proliferated, prices soared. The average rate increase for a business seeking to renew coverage in the fourth quarter of 2001 was nearly 30 percent. Reinsurance prices rose sharply as well. Very little private sector coverage for terrorism entered the market as a general consensus emerged that terrorism risk is fundamentally not insurable. Insurers, who are regulated by the states, therefore took the unprecedented step of seeking financial protection from the federal government in the event of future attacks. Only when the Terrorism Risk Insurance Act (TRIA) was enacted by Congress in November 2002—fourteen months after the attack—did stability finally return to the market and coverage for terrorist attacks resume.

Changes in the Terrorism Threat Landscape and Impacts on Terrorism Insurance Markets

In the immediate aftermath of 9/11 the ability of commercial policyholders to purchase adequate limits of terrorism coverage at affordable prices was severely constrained. Commercial property owners and businesses were faced with substantially reduced protection for terrorism-related risks, in addition to higher property/casualty rates overall. As a result, many were forced to go without coverage or only partly insure their assets.

Today, reports of property owners having problems securing terrorism coverage due to a lack of capacity in the market are no longer making headline news. Indeed, it is therefore tempting to conclude that in the ten years since TRIA was first implemented that insurance markets have fully adjusted to the post-9/11 environment and that insurers and reinsurers have concluded that terrorism is a fully insurance risk.

The reality is quite different. The fact of the matter is that terrorism risk today is almost every bit as uninsurable as it was a decade ago. Recent major successes in the war on terror, including the killing of al-Qaida leader Osama bin Laden in 2011, do not alter this conclusion. This is because the current stability in the terrorism insurance market in the United States is due almost entirely to two factors:

1. There has been no successful terrorist attack on U.S. soil since 2001, and
2. TRIA remains in place.

The influence of both of these factors is discussed in the sections that follow.

Absence of Successful Attacks Does Not Imply Terrorism Risk is Inconsequential

The fact that there has been no successful terrorist attack in the United States in eleven years is a remarkable achievement. It is a testimony to the hard work and dedication of this nation's counterterrorism agencies and the bravery of the men and women in uniform who fought and continue to fight battles abroad to keep us safe here at home.

Unfortunately, the threat from terrorist attack in the United States is both real and substantial and will remain as such for the foreseeable future. Indeed, the U.S. State Department warned in a recent report that despite the death of bin Laden and other key al-Qaida figures, the terrorist network's affiliates and adherents remain adaptable and resilient, and constitute "an enduring and serious threat to our national security."[3]

Table 1 below shows that interest in attacking targets within the United States remains undiminished. Indeed, it is clear from Table 1 that in addition to an ongoing threat from foreign terrorist networks, the United States also faces homegrown (domestic) terrorist threats from radical individuals, who may be inspired by al-Qaida and others, but may have little or no actual connection to militant groups.

Catastrophe modeler Risk Management Solutions (RMS) points to an increase in the number of homegrown plots in the U.S. in recent years.4 Many of these have been thwarted, such as the attempt by Najibullah Zazi to bomb the New York subway system and Mohamed Osman Mohamud who targeted a Portland, Oregon, Christmas tree lighting ceremony. Also among the more notable unsuccessful attacks was a 2010 attempted car bomb attack in New York City's Times Square. Other thwarted attacks against passenger and cargo aircraft, including the Christmas Day 2009 attempt to blowup a jet over Detroit, are indicative of an ongoing risk to aviation infrastructure.

Table 1. Recent Terrorist Attack Attempts In The U.S.

Date	Location	Event
August, 2012	Ludowici, GA	Four U.S. soldiers charged in connection with murder and illegal gang activity, linked to foiled plot to commit domestic acts of terrorism, including overthrowing the government and assassinating the President
May, 2012	TBD	Foiled underwear bomb plot to bring down U.S.-bound commercial airliner around the anniversary of bin Laden's death
July 27, 2011	Fort Hood, TX	U.S. Army Pfc Naser Jason Abdo arrested and charged with plotting bomb attack on fellow soldiers at Fort Hood, TX
June 22, 2011	Seattle, WA	Two men arrested in plot to attack military recruiting station in Seattle
May 11, 2011	New York City, NY	Ahmed Ferhani and Mohamed Mamdouh arrested in plot to attack Manhattan synagogue
February 23, 2011	Lubbock, TX	Foiled plot to bomb military and political targets, including former President George W. Bush in New York, Colorado and California
December 8, 2010	Baltimore, MD	Attempted bombing of Armed Forces recruiting center by U.S. citizen Antonio Martinez, aka Muhammad Hussain
November 26, 2010	Portland, OR	Attempted bombing at Christmas tree lighting ceremony in downtown Portland by naturalized U.S. citizen Mohamed Osman Mohamud
October, 2010	Washington D.C.	Attempted plot to bomb D.C.-area metro stations
May 1, 2010	New York City, NY	Attempted SUV bombing in Times Square, New York City, by naturalized U.S. citizen Faisal Shahzad
December 25, 2009	Over Detroit, MI	Attempted bombing of Northwest Airlines passenger jet over Detroit by underwear bomber Umar Farouk Abdulmutallab
September, 2009	New York City, NY	U.S. resident Najibullah Zazi and others charged with conspiracy to use weapons of mass destruction in New York City
September, 2009	Springfield, IL	Attempted plot to detonate a vehicle bomb at the federal building in Springfield, IL
September, 2009	Dallas, TX	Attempted bombing of skyscraper in Dallas, TX
May, 2009	New York City, NY	Foiled plot to bomb Jewish synagogue and shoot down military planes in New York City
May, 2009	Various U.S. targets	Conviction of Liberty City six for conspiring to plan attacks on U.S. targets, including Sears Tower, Chicago

Source: Federal Bureau of Investigation (FBI); various news reports; Insurance Information Institute.

Table 1 also demonstrates that the threat of terrorism is not confined to the country's largest cities such as New York and Washington. Recent attempted attacks have occurred in medium and small metropolitan areas including Portland, Oregon, in Lubbock, Texas and Springfield, Illinois.

Another evolving threat is cyber-terrorism. Recent high profile attacks, such as the sabotaging of Iran's nuclear program via the Stuxnet computer worm and malicious infiltration attempts here in the U.S. by foreign entities, underscore the growing threat to both national security and the economy.

All these factors suggest that terrorism risk will be a constant and evolving threat for the foreseeable future.

THE FEDERAL ROLE: IMPACT OF TRIA IN MAINTAINING INSURANCE MARKET STABILITY

Without question, TRIA and its successors are the principal reason for the continued stability in the insurance and reinsurance market for terrorism insurance today. As discussed previously, TRIA is credited with restoring terrorism coverage in commercial insurance policies upon its enactment in late 2002.

It is worth noting that in 2004, more than a year before the original Act's expiration at year-end 2005, terrorism exclusions once again emerged for policies with exposure extending into 2006. This was an unmistakable indication that insurance and reinsurance markets felt that terrorism risk, at least for larger scale attacks, remained uninsurable in the private sector. After Congress agreed to extend the program for another two years under the Terrorism Risk Insurance Extension Act of 2005 (TRIEA), terrorism coverage remained available and affordable in the market. However, with TRIEA's looming expiration in year-end 2006, terrorism exclusions once again appeared in the market, signaling the market's assessment that terrorism risk remained fundamentally uninsurable. These exclusions largely disappeared following passage of a 7-year extension of the program under the Terrorism Risk Insurance Program Reauthorization Act of 2007 (TRIPRA). With TRIPRA's expiration now a little more than two years away (year-end 2014), it is virtually certain that terrorism exclusions will reappear in the market in 2013. Indeed, insurance broker Aon estimates that at least 80 percent of the commercial property market will be impacted by these exclusions and other restrictions.

Studies by various organizations, including the University of Pennsylvania's Wharton School Risk Center, the RAND Corporation and the Organization for Economic Cooperation and Development (OECD), have supported the idea of a substantive federal role in terrorism insurance. In particular, the Wharton School found that TRIA has had a positive effect on availability of terrorism coverage and also has significantly contributed to reducing insurance premiums.[5] The OECD notes, however, that the financial (capital) markets have thus far shown little appetite for terrorism risk.

Evidence from Other Countries: Terrorism Risk Insurance Programs Abroad

Additional evidence that terrorism risk is fundamentally uninsurable comes from abroad. A number of countries have established their own terrorism risk insurance programs and these have operated successfully, often for many years. Australia, Austria, Belgium, France, Germany, the Netherlands, Spain, Switzerland and the United Kingdom have all created programs to cover terrorism in the event of an attack on their own soil.[6]

This begs the question as to why—eleven years after the 9/11 attack and a decade after the initial terrorism risk insurance program legislation was enacted—terrorism risk, particularly for large-scale attacks, is still viewed as uninsurable? The answer is surprisingly simple and explains why even the absence of a successful major attack on U.S. soil since 2001 does not alter this assessment.

OBSTACLES TO INSURING LOSSES ARISING FROM ACTS OF TERRORISM

Simply put, acts of terror violate all four of the basic requirements traditionally associated with insurability of a risk. In situations where these requirements cannot be met, it is difficult or impossible to ascertain the premium to be charged and/or difficult or impossible to achieve the necessary spread of risk to avoid excessive exposure to catastrophic loss, thereby threatening the insurer's solvency. Consequently, such a risk would generally be deemed to be commercially not viable (i.e., insurable) in whole or in part.

The four basic requirements for insurability of a risk are detailed below (as well in Exhibits 3A and 3B), with a description of how terrorism risk violates each requirement:

1. *Estimable Frequency*: Insurers require a large number of observations to develop predictive, statistically sound rate-making models (an actuarial concept known as "credibility"). For example, insurers handle millions of auto, home, workers compensation and business property claims every year, providing them with vast amounts of data from which they can reliably estimate the frequency of such claims. For major catastrophic risks such as hurricanes and earthquakes that occur less frequently insurers still maintain databases with hundreds or even thousands of these events, supplemented by sophisticated catastrophe models, that help provide statistically reliable estimates of frequency. Terrorism risk is clearly different in this respect.

   Obstacle: There are very few data points on which to base frequency estimates for acts of terror in the United States, thus estimates lack any true actuarial credibility. The opinions of experts on the likelihood of terrorist attacks, which might be viewed by some as substitutes for actuarially credible data, are also highly subjective. At any given time, there is a wide range of viewpoints among national security experts on the likelihood, location and/or attack modality. Moreover, insurers have no access to data used internally by counterterrorism agencies. Given the paucity of historical data and diversity and shifting nature of expert opinions, catastrophe models used to estimate terrorism risk are relatively undeveloped compared to those used to assess natural hazard risks. The bottom line is that estimating the frequency of terror attacks with any degree of accuracy (credibility) is extraordinarily challenging, if not impossible in many circumstances.

2. *Estimable Severity:* Insurability requires that the maximum possible/probable loss be estimable in order to calculate the insurer's exposure (in dollar terms) and minimize its "probability of ruin." No insurer can expose itself to losses of a magnitude that present an unreasonable risk of insolvency.

   Obstacle: Potential losses arising from terrorist attacks are virtually unbounded. In this sense terrorism risk is akin to war risk, which is almost universally excluded from commercial insurance policies worldwide. Consequently, losses arising from acts of terror can easily exceed an insurer's claims paying capital resources. Workers compensation coverage, which does not permit any exclusions or limitation if injuries or deaths arise from terrorist acts, can lead to extreme losses that on their own could potentially bankrupt an insurer under some attack scenarios. In addition, when it comes to estimating losses from potential terrorist attacks there also appears to be significant variability in outcomes (i.e., disagreement on estimated severity impacts), underscoring the degree of uncertainty associated with potential terrorist attacks.

3. *Diversifiable Risk:* Insurability requires that the losses can be spread across a large number of risks. This is an application of the "Law of Large Numbers" and helps makes losses more manageable and less volatile. Failure to achieve an adequate spread of risk increases the risk of insolvency in the same way that an undiversified portfolio of stocks (or any asset) is riskier than a well-diversified portfolio.

4. *Obstacle:* Terrorism attacks are likely to be highly concentrated geographically (e.g., World Trade Center site), concentrated within an industry (e.g., power plants, airports) or within a certain span of time (e.g., coordinated attack).

   Random Loss Distribution/Fortuity: Insurability requires that the probability of a loss occurring be random or fortuitous. This implies that individual events must be unpredictable in terms of timing, location and magnitude.

   Obstacle: Terrorism attacks are planned, coordinated and deliberate acts of destruction. Again, they are likely to be highly concentrated geographically (e.g., World Trade Center site) or concentrated within an industry (e.g., power plants). Terrorists engage in "dynamic target shifting" whereby terrorists shift from "hardened targets" to "soft targets" which implies that losses are not random or fortuitous in nature.

THE SUCCESS OF THE TERRORISM RISK INSURANCE PROGRAM

The Terrorism Risk Insurance Program, by all objective measures, is a success. The program not only succeeded in restoring stability to the country's vital insurance and reinsurance markets in the wake of the unprecedented market dislocations associated with the September 11, 2001 terrorist attack, but it continues to deliver substantive, direct benefits to businesses, workers, consumers and the economy overall—all at little or no cost to taxpayers.

Availability and Affordability

One measure of success is the "take-up rate" (i.e., share or businesses purchasing coverage) of insurance coverage among. Insurance brokers Marsh and Aon both estimate that take-up rates for terrorism coverage are in the 60% to 65% range over the past several years (ranging as high as 80% in some industries), up from approximately 27% in 2003—the first full year under TRIA. This suggests that coverage is widely available, is affordable and is routinely purchased in the market. It is important to note, however, that the take-up rate for workers compensation coverage is effectively 100%. This is because workers compensation is a compulsory (all employers must purchase coverage) combined with the fact that states do not allow exclusions for terrorism losses in workers compensation programs.

Affordable pricing is another measure of the program's success. While pricing varies across industries, reflecting differences in risk, the average commercial terrorism premium is equivalent to approximately 0.5% of a company's total insured value, according to brokers. Prices can also be stated as a share of the cost of the insured's total insurance program, in which case annual premiums account for approximately 5% to 6% of total costs, again varying by industry.

Capacity

One primary goal of TRIA and it successors has been to encourage private sector capacity to enter (and remain) in the marketplace so that an increasing share of losses from future terrorist attacks could be borne in the private sector.

Evidence of the program's success in this respect has been documented by a number of government entities and other organizations. In its latest report on terrorism risk insurance market conditions, the President's Working Group on Financial Markets noted that the program provides an incentive to property/casualty insurers and reinsurers who might not otherwise provide terrorism insurance at current capacity levels or prices.[7] The U.S. Government

Accountability Office (GAO), commenting on the availability and affordability of terrorism coverage in large metropolitan areas, reported that with a few exceptions, commercial property terrorism insurance appears to be available nationwide at rates policyholders believe is reasonable, suggesting ample capacity.[8]

Note that this statement is very different from an assessment that such capacity would exist in the absence of a terrorism backstop. Again, it is important to emphasize that the majority of the coverage that exists in the market today exists because of the continued existence of the Terrorism Risk Insurance Program. As noted earlier, insurance broker Aon estimates that 70% to 80% of the market would encounter terrorism exclusions if the program were discontinued. Thus capacity in the market is largely contingent upon the continuation of the program.

The so-called market for "standalone" terrorism coverage also provides evidence that in the absence of a Terrorism Risk Insurance Program, coverage capacity (supply) will fall well short of demand. Insurance brokers Marsh and Aon both report that the "theoretical" maximum amount of coverage available per risk in the "standalone" market is approximately $2 billion with larger sums available under some circumstances. This is in contrast with limits of just $150 million or less available in early 2002 before TRIA was enacted. At the time, such coverage also was subject to high deductibles equal to 7 to 10 percent of the stated value of the coverage.[9] While the sums available in the market today may seem large, especially in comparison to 2002, there are many risks for which the coverage is inadequate. Consider, for example, that back in 2001 (prior to the introduction of terrorism exclusions) the twin towers at the World Trade Center site were insured for $3.55 billion—more than what is generally available in the market today. Multibillion dollars risks are now quite common in the United States, from office and shopping complexes to large manufacturing facilities, sports stadiums, transportation hubs and energy infrastructure not to mention infrastructure such as bridges, tunnels and dams.

Reinsurance capacity, which was extremely limited in the aftermath of 9/11, is up as well. A 2011 report from reinsurance broker Guy Carpenter noted that there is between $6 billion and $8 billion of terrorism reinsurance capacity available in the U.S. market, but cautions that the market remains vulnerable to a major terrorism loss. This caution is appropriate. Indeed, many modeled loss scenarios result in insured losses in the tens or even hundreds of billions of dollars—some even exceeding the claims paying capital of the entire industry. As noted previously, much of the capacity in the market today is predicated on the existence of the Terrorism Risk Insurance Program. In the absence of the program, reinsurance capacity would be greatly reduced.

FACTORS THAT COULD INFLUENCE GREATER PRIVATE SECTOR PARTICIPATION IN THE TERRORISM INSURANCE MARKETPLACE

As discussed previously, the primary factor influencing private sector participation in the market for terrorism insurance, apart from the absence of a successful attack on U.S. soil since 2001, is the continued existence of the Terrorism Risk Insurance Program. The program's success to date has stabilized insurance and reinsurance markets, enhanced availability and affordability of coverage and encouraged private sector capacity to enter the market, thereby helping businesses invest, grow and create jobs. What follows are several options, based on international experience and U.S. experience to date, that could potentially further increase private sector participation in the markets for terrorism insurance and reinsurance.

Long-Term Extension or Permanence of a Terrorism Risk Insurance Program

The positive experience of other countries, some of which have had programs in place much longer than the United States, combined with favorable recent U.S. experience under the current 7-year extension of the program under TRIPRA, suggests that a longterm extension—or a decision to make the program permanent—could be an effective means to achieve increased private sector participation in the program. If insurers and reinsurers are assured that the program will be in place for the indefinite future, uncertainty is reduced. From an economic perspective, the reduction in uncertainty would likely be conducive for investment under the program.

Pooling Proposal

As Congress begins to explore alternatives to enhance private sector participation in the market for terrorism risk, it is instructive to recall that insurers began their effort to create a federal "backstop" very shortly after the September 11 attacks. By late September 2001, insurers had already drafted an outline describing their plan for a federal backstop and legislation was drafted in early October. Dubbed the "Insurance Stabilization and Availability Act of 2001," the bill proposed the establishment of a privately run and financed terrorism reinsurance pool, organized as a federally-chartered mutual insurance company, that would reinsure the terrorism risks of U.S. licensed insurers and reinsurers and purchase reinsurance from the federal government in exchange for a premium. The organizational structure of the pool would have been similar to that of Pool Reinsurance Company Ltd. (often referred to as "Pool Re"), a mutual insurer established in Great Britain in 1993 after several bombings attributed to the Irish Republican Army (IRA) made insurers reluctant to offer coverage for terrorist acts (Pool Re now provides coverage against a broad range of terrorism risks). While no doubt adjustments would need to be made given the passage of more than a decade since the industry's initial pooling proposal, the concept of a pool has worked successfully in the U.K. for 20 years.

SUMMARY

In the eleven years since the tragedy of the September 11, 2001 terrorist attack on the United States, much has been learned about the nature of terrorism risk and its insurability. There is no question that the Terrorism Risk Insurance Act and its successors brought much needed stability to the market in the aftermath of the most costly insurance loss in global history. In the decade since, private sector insurers, reinsurers and the federal government have successfully partnered with one another in order to maintain that stability, providing tangible benefits for businesses large and small—and their employees—all across America.

The looming expiration of the TRIPRA at the end of 2014 brings to a head the question of whether terrorism risk is now, or ever will be, a risk that can be managed entirely within the private sector. The evidence, both in the United States and from similar programs abroad, is that market stability in terms of both pricing and availability of terrorism coverage, as well as the ability to maintain adequate and expanding levels of capacity over time, are contingent on the continued existence of the Terrorism Risk Insurance Program.

Thank you for you for the opportunity to testify before the Committee today. I would be happy to respond to any questions you may have.

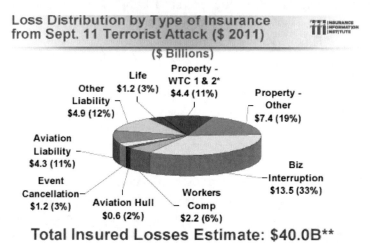

Total Insured Losses Estimate: $40.0B**

*Loss total does not include March 2010 New York City settlement of up to $657.5 million to compensate approximately 10,000 Ground Zero workers or any subsequent settlements.

**$32.5 billion in 2001 dollars.

Exhibit 1.

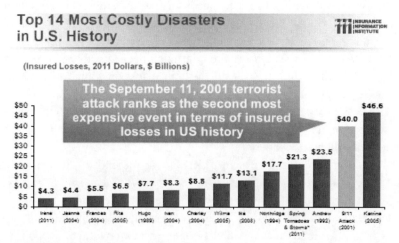

Sources: PCS; Insurance Information Institute inflation adjustments.
Note: Property losses only except in the case of 9/11, which includes all impacted lines. 9/11 property losses totaled $23.5 billion.

Exhibit 2.

Terrorism Violates Traditional Requirements for Insurability

Requirement	Definition	Violation
Estimable Frequency	•Insurance requires large number of observations to develop predictive rate-making models (an actuarial concept known as credibility)	•Very few data points •Terror modeling still in infancy, untested. •Inconsistent assessment of threat
Estimable Severity	•Maximum possible/ probable loss must be at least estimable in order to minimize "risk of ruin" (insurer cannot run an unreasonable risk of insolvency though assumption of the risk)	•Potential loss is virtually unbounded. •Losses can easily exceed insurer capital resources for paying claims. •Extreme risk in workers compensation and statute forbids exclusions.

Source: Insurance Information Institute.

Exhibit 3A.

Terrorism Violates Traditional Requirements for Insurability (cont'd)

Requirement	Definition	Violation
Diversifiable Risk	•Must be able to spread/distribute risk across large number of risks •"Law of Large Numbers" helps makes losses manageable and less volatile	•Losses likely highly concentrated geographically or by industry (e.g., WTC, power plants)
Random Loss Distribution/ Fortuity	•Probability of loss occurring must be purely random and fortuitous •Events are individually unpredictable in terms of time, location and magnitude	•Terrorism attacks are planned, coordinated and deliberate acts of destruction •Dynamic target shifting from "hardened targets" to "soft targets" •Terrorist adjust tactics to circumvent new security measures •Actions of US and foreign govts. may affect likelihood, nature and timing of attack

Source: Insurance Information Institute

Exhibit 3B.

End Notes

[1] Contact information: Tel: (212) 346-5520; Email: bobh@iii.org.

[2] The loss totals do not include the March 2010 settlement of up to $657.5 million announced by New York City officials and plaintiffs' lawyers to compensate about 10,000 workers whose health was damaged during the rescue and cleanup at the World Trade Center.

[3] Country Reports on Terrorism 2011, U.S. Department of State, July 31, 2012.

[4] RMS Terrorism Risk Briefing, July 2012.

[5] Evaluating the Effectiveness of Terrorism Risk Financing Solutions, Howard C. Kunreuther and Erwann O. Michel-Kerjan, September 2007, National Bureau of Economic Research.

[6] In 1993, the British government formed a mutual reinsurance pool for terrorist coverage following acts of terrorism by the Irish Republican Army. Insurance companies pay premiums at rates set by the pool. The primary insurer pays the entire claim for terrorist damage but is reimbursed by the pool for losses in excess of a certain amount per event and per year based on its share of the total market. Following 9/11, coverage was extended to cover all risks, except war, including nuclear and biological contamination, aircraft impact and flooding, if caused by terrorist attacks. The British government acts as the reinsurer of last resort, guaranteeing payments above the industry retention.

[7] Market Conditions for Terrorism Risk Insurance 2010, Report of the President's Working Group on Financial Markets.

[8] Initial Results on Availability of Terrorism Insurance in Specific Geographic Markets, GAO-08-919R, July 2008.

[9] September 11, 2001: One Hundred Minutes of Terror that Changed the Global Insurance Industry Forever, Robert P. Hartwig, John Liner Review, January 2002.

In: Terrorism Risk Insurance   ISBN: 978-1-62618-697-2
Editor: Oscar A. Madsen   © 2013 Nova Science Publishers, Inc.

Chapter 3

TESTIMONY OF DAVID C. JOHN, SENIOR RESEARCH FELLOW, THE HERITAGE FOUNDATION. HEARING ON "TRIA AT TEN YEARS: THE FUTURE OF THE TERRORISM RISK INSURANCE PROGRAM"[*]

TRIA: TIME TO END THE PROGRAM

Chairman Biggert and Ranking Member Gutierrez, thank you for inviting me to participate in this hearing. I am David C. John, the Senior Research Fellow in Retirement Security and Financial Institutions at The Heritage Foundation. The views I express in this testimony are my own, and should not be construed as representing any official position of The Heritage Foundation.

The Terrorism Risk Insurance Act (TRIA) served a very real purpose in the days after 9/11 when insurance companies and their customers feared the cost of providing coverage for acts of terrorism would be prohibitive. However, we have now reached a point where the private sector is increasingly capable of providing that coverage at appropriate prices without government support. In fact, the continued existence of TRIA may keep the

---

[*] This is an edited, reformatted and augmented version of a testimony presented September 11, 2012 before the House Committee on Financial Services, Subcommittee on Insurance, Housing and Community Opportunity.

industry from further progress. However, the industry will need time to make the transition to a fully private terrorism system, and it is greatly to the Subcommittee's credit that you are beginning to discuss this issue now instead of waiting until closer to the program's 2014 expiration date.

Back in 2001, TRIA served a real purpose. Without swift but well-considered action from Congress, thousands of American businesses might have been unable to continue purchasing affordable terrorism insurance. The massive losses from the September 11, 2001 attacks made property and casualty insurers understandably reluctant to continue to issue property insurance policies that included terrorism coverage until they could evaluate their exposure to potential terrorist attacks. They were equally reluctant to issue stand-alone policies that only covered acts of terrorism.

Before TRIA, property and casualty insurers faced a serious dilemma. Many of their corporate policies issued before the 9/11 attacks insured against terrorist attacks in much the same way they covered natural disasters or more conventional accidents. Then and now, insurance premiums on most types of loss were based on sophisticated estimates of the likelihood that a particular claim will have to be paid. Until September 11, insurers never expected the scale of damage inflicted in those attacks. Thus before 9/11, terrorism coverage often carried a very low price tag and often was included without much additional though in more comprehensive coverage.

Then the world changed. Insurers and the rest of us discovered that such attacks were possible and could cause catastrophic damage. At the time, none of us had any firm idea whether those attacks were isolated incidents or not. As a result, they were unable to price terrorism coverage quickly and accurately, and unwilling to expose their companies to claims that could run in the tens of billions of dollars.

Losses from the World Trade Center attacks were spread among many foreign and domestic insurers and "reinsurers." This is standard practice for large policies; insurers essentially spread the risk among many other companies in return for a share of the premiums generated by the policies. Some of the risk is sold to reinsurers, who generally insure the insurance companies against huge losses. In this way, no one company is left facing ruin when there is a huge claim on a policy. This method enabled the industry to absorb the roughly $35 billion in claims from the attacks on the World Trade Center. However, in the days after 9/11, many insurers and reinsurers that would have had great difficulty paying another such loss were unwilling to renew policies that include terrorism coverage.

As we knew at the time, the wrong government response could prevent the market from taking the necessary actions. Any program that essentially transferred the risk from companies to the government by promising that tax dollars would pay most of the losses would only make it more difficult for private insurers to establish the real market price for terrorism coverage. Because the industry would be collecting premiums without facing the true value of potential losses, such coverage would be underpriced. Those who bought this insurance would not have any incentive to reduce their risk, but every incentive to support extending the federal program indefinitely.

While the problem in 2001 was real, it should have been temporary. By now, normal insurance industry processes should have already been able to resolve it. The industry should have developed ways to price terrorism coverage properly, which could include upper limits on company liability. And reinsurers should have found ways to involve sophisticated investors who, for a price, could face the type of losses that could occur.

Recent industry data indicates that there has been a great deal of progress towards making terrorism coverage both widely available and affordable. While coverage varies according to geographic area and industry, some industries show that over three-quarters of larger firms have purchased some form of terrorism coverage. In addition, the cost appears to be declining, with one major report suggesting that the cost dropped by almost a third between 2008 and 2009 alone. Clearly, the process is well underway, and Congress should remove the last barriers to restoring full private coverage for acts of terrorism by ending TRIA.

The recession has had a negative effect on the number of firms that have been able to renew their coverage, but this is to be expected. Faced with cash flow problems, firms will cut wherever that can. What is concerning is that industry sources suggest that the risk models used for terrorism insurance are still more primitive than those used for other types of catastrophic coverage. This may well be due to the continued presence of TRIA, which limits a firms risk exposure and may cause them to focus more on the risk that the firm retains than on the potential losses that the government would cover.

TRIA was not intended to be a permanent program. As the original bill stated, TRIA would "provide temporary financial compensation to insured parties, contributing to the stabilization of the United States economy in a time of national crisis, while the financial services industry develops the systems, mechanisms, products, and programs necessary to create a viable financial services market for private terrorism risk insurance." Returning this coverage to the private sector is an important goal, because there is no reason why taxpayers should continue to have the ultimate financial responsibility for paying insurance losses on private property. The insurance crisis has passed, and the insurance industry now has enough information about terrorist attacks to again provide this coverage. As a result, there is no reason to extend TRIA beyond its scheduled 2014 expiration date.

Some insurance industry associations and others argue that without TRIA, terrorism coverage will revert to some level of problems, but this should not be the case. By 2014, the industry should have over 12 years of data that would allow it to appropriately price its coverage. If, and let me stress the if, the industry cannot assume total responsibility, Congress should start the process in early 2013 by implementing proposals such as increasing the deductible to be paid by insurers, increasing the insurer co-participation, increasing the event trigger, removing coverage for acts of domestic terrorism; and reducing the recoupment percentage from 133 percent to 100 percent. These changes should take effect almost as soon as they can be passed.

That should be followed by a full phase-out of TRIA so that the entire program has ended no more than two years after the current 2014 expiration date. If these steps are necessary, Congress should also strongly indicate to the industry that further extensions will not come, and that it should expect to offer terrorism coverage after that without any further taxpayer subsidies.

Let It Expire

Congress should neither extend nor expand TRIA without a firm and short phaseout, and if Congress passes any longer extension, whoever is in the White House after January 20 should reject such legislation. Continuing to pass the risk of property insurance losses caused by terrorist attacks to taxpayers does nothing to increase security. Rather, programs like TRIA encourage insurance companies to avoid the proper pricing of coverage, with the expectation that federal reinsurance under TRIA will enable them to pass on significant losses to taxpayers. TRIA is thus a pre-approved bailout for insurance companies, the essence of corporate welfare. There was a good reason to establish TRIA, but those days are over. TRIA has served its purpose and should now be allowed to expire.

In: Terrorism Risk Insurance
Editor: Oscar A. Madsen

ISBN: 978-1-62618-697-2
© 2013 Nova Science Publishers, Inc.

Chapter 4

STATEMENT OF ROLF LUNDBERG, SENIOR VICE PRESIDENT, CONGRESSIONAL AND PUBLIC AFFAIRS, U.S. CHAMBER OF COMMERCE. HEARING ON "TRIA AT TEN YEARS: THE FUTURE OF THE TERRORISM RISK INSURANCE PROGRAM"*

Good morning, Chairwoman Biggert, Ranking Member Gutierrez, and members of the Subcommittee. I appreciate the opportunity to testify today regarding the important issue of terrorism risk insurance and its importance to the economy. My name is Rolf Lundberg, and I am the Senior Vice President for Congressional and Public Affairs at the U.S. Chamber of Commerce. The U.S. Chamber of Commerce is the world's largest business federation representing the interests of more than 3 million businesses of all sizes, sectors, and regions, as well as state and local chambers and industry associations.

I am appearing today on behalf of the Coalition to Insure Against Terrorism (CIAT), of which the U.S. Chamber is a member. CIAT is a broad coalition of commercial insurance consumers formed immediately after 9/11 to ensure that American businesses could obtain comprehensive and affordable terrorism insurance. CIAT's membership of 79 major trade and membership

---

* This is an edited, reformatted and augmented version of a Statement Presented September 11, 2012 before the House Committee on Financial Services, Subcommittee on Insurance, Housing and Community Opportunity.

associations, representing virtually every sector of the economy, has remained resolute from the original proposal through the 2005 and 2007 reauthorizations and now, in recognizing, as did Congress and the Administration, that only the Federal government could provide the framework to make this coverage available to all those who required it to invest on new construction and to carry on commerce. The diverse CIAT membership represents commercial real estate, banking, energy, construction, hotel and hospitality, entertainment, manufacturing, transportation, the major league sports, as well as public sector buyers of insurance. CIAT is the true consumer voice on terrorism risk insurance, as we are comprised of the principal policyholders of commercial property and casualty lines of insurance in the United States.

I am pleased today to offer the policyholder perspective on terrorism risk insurance, and to highlight why the TRIA program continues to be vital to our economy. As we saw in the months following the 9/11 terrorist attacks, the lack of terrorism risk insurance contributed to a paralysis in the economy, especially in construction, tourism, business travel and real estate finance. Enactment of TRIA changed that by making terrorism risk coverage widely available to commercial policyholders, and delivering it through a private insurance mechanism that keeps the private industry's skin in the game through the insurer deductible and co-share layers. It also protects taxpayers by providing recoupment -- from us the commercial policyholders -- of any federal share paid out in the wake of a large-scale terrorist event. While private insurance capacity apparently has grown slightly in the past decade, these years have also taught us that a continuing federal role in this unique risk remains vital. The terrorism peril is simply too intrinsically linked to government policy and intelligence to be solely handled by the private sector alone. TRIA needs to be reauthorized, and we therefore commend you, Chairwoman Biggert and the Subcommittee, for your leadership on this issue and for convening this important hearing.

The 26 foot tall banner that stretches across the front of the U.S. Chamber of Commerce headquarters in Washington, D.C., spells out our nation's biggest challenge and our highest priority in one word—J-O-B-S. That banner has served as a reminder to us and to all of Washington of where our focus must be.

The Chamber believes that stronger and faster economic growth is the best way to successfully put Americans back to work. We must not only affirmatively clear away impediments to job creation, but we must avoid taking steps that would create more uncertainty and strangle businesses, stifling our economy's ability to grow, and also negatively affect job creation.

At the same time as we seek to remove barriers that will allow businesses to invest and grow, we also have to recognize what policies work – policies that allow business to continue to invest and look ahead and have confidence in the future.

We know from previous experience following 9/11 that the impact on jobs of the absence of terrorism insurance was widespread and growing. Our economy today is more than 20% larger than it was a decade ago. There is every reason to expect that the jobs impact would be greater and more widespread today were the certainty of the terrorism insurance program to be pulled out from under our economy.

America has strong demographics, abundant natural resources, the world's most productive workers, and a long history of picking ourselves up when we are down. We should not self-inflict additional and unnecessary damage to our fragile economy, and possibility extinguish the prospect of economic recovery and new jobs for Americans.

With this in mind, I would like to focus my remarks today on three main areas: (1) the importance of terrorism risk insurance to the broader economy; (2) how and why the TRIA program continues to serve an important purpose; and (3) the current state of the terrorism risk insurance market.

THE IMPORTANCE OF TERRORISM INSURANCE TO THE ECONOMY

On today's solemn anniversary we remember the thousands of innocent lives lost on that tragic day eleven years ago, and offer our thoughts and prayers to the families and loved ones left behind. The terrorists who perpetrated that terrible attack intended to paralyze us with fear -- but the best of America shone through that day, and in the weeks and months that followed.

It is incumbent upon us to remember the lessons of 9/11. Among those lessons is the importance of maintaining safeguards to ensure that such catastrophic events do not cause lasting harm to our economy. As we saw in the months that followed 9/11, managing the risk of terrorism is an imperative. It was a critical situation: it was difficult, if not impossible, for commercial policyholders to secure coverage against terrorism risk, yet banks and other capital providers would not provide financing without it. In 14 months between the 9/11 attack and enactment of TRIA, over $15 billion in real estate related transactions were stalled or even cancelled because of a lack of terrorism risk insurance, according to a Real Estate Roundtable study. Furthermore, the White House Council of Economic Advisors found that there was an immediate and direct loss of 300,000 jobs in that period from deferred construction investment.

The simple fact is that our recovery from 9/11 was slowed due to a lack of any realistic solution for the private sector to manage terrorism risk. Furthermore, our ability to recover from a further attack was also severely weakened by the situation. The months following 9/11 made clear that a strong, resilient economy requires a plan to deal with potentially devastating terrorism losses. Indeed, several other nations have terrorism insurance programs, including several that pre-date TRIA. Undoubtedly, we would face the same post-9/11 danger to our economy if Congress were to let the TRIA backstop expire without replacing it with a permanent solution.

THE TERRORISM RISK INSURANCE ACT

In recognition of the critical post-9/11 situation, Congress and the Bush Administration worked together in 2002 to enact TRIA -- a public-private partnership to deal with terrorism risk that has served our nation and its economy well for nearly 10 years. The TRIA program has a dual purpose: (1) to keep our economy functioning smoothly by requiring private insurers to make terrorism coverage available to commercial policyholders; and (2) to provide an efficient mechanism for managing terrorism losses in a way that maximizes private sector involvement and provides strong protection for taxpayers.

As commercial policyholders, we are well versed in the benefits of TRIA's first purpose, i.e., the "make available" provision. We have no interest in seeing a return to the standard terrorism exclusions became the norm in the months following 9/11. In fact, when TRIA was originally set to expire in 2005, and again in 2007, we saw policy renewals with "springing exclusions" that would have voided terrorism coverage upon expiration of the program. Having TRIA in place, quite simply, has been difference between being able to manage terrorism risk or holding one's breath.

Policyholders understand that the reason terrorism coverage is available is because of the TRIA backstop. However, to view the TRIA program as simply a federal backstop is to miss key components of the program. In truth, the TRIA program is a public-private partnership where all parties participate in managing risk. Private insurers take a large share of losses through both the insurer deductible and through the 15% co-share of any losses exceeding the deductible. The federal government steps in only in certain, severe cases, where losses from the terrorist event exceed $100 million, and only then if an insurer has losses that exceed its statutory deductible. We policyholders also bear substantial costs, in the form of the premiums we pay for terrorism coverage, and through the responsibility for paying post-event surcharges so that taxpayers may recoup federal assistance provided through the backstop.

The simple reality is that having TRIA in place actually saves the taxpayers money. As currently structured, the program is only likely to trigger federal compensation in truly massive, catastrophic terrorism events. In the absence of TRIA, such an event would likely cause Congress to appropriate millions, if not billions, in ad hoc disaster assistance, with no strings attached. Under TRIA, however, there is a pre-existing mechanism to ensure economic recovery -- a mechanism that maximizes which private sector involvement, and protects taxpayers through the recoupment provision.

CURRENT MARKET CONDITIONS

Because of TRIA, today terrorism risk insurance (with one exception) is generally available for commercial policyholders. It would not be available without TRIA. CIAT members have generally seen a decline in pricing for terrorism insurance, which we attribute not just to the normal ebb and flow of the insurance market, but rather to the continued availability of the TRIA backstop and the fact that there have been no certified acts of terrorism since the enactment of TRIA.

Even with TRIA, however, we note that coverage for nuclear, biological, chemical and radiological ("NBCR") events remains extremely limited in terms of availability and affordability. Where insurers do offer such coverage, it may be limited in terms of geographic area (*i.e.*, coverage is harder to procure in perceived "target" cities such as New York or Washington), and it may also be limited to certain perils (*i.e.*, biological and chemical events may be covered, but not nuclear or radiological). Coverage limits for NBCR insurance that is available tend to be relatively low and expensive.

We understand that the principal factor in insurers' decisions not to cover NBCR is their lack of sufficient data to properly model their exposure to such losses with any degree of certainty. On this point, we would point out that this Committee has previously considered measures intended to encourage greater availability and affordability of NBCR coverage, though they were not ultimately included in the TRIA reauthorization legislation. We believe that policymakers may need to revisit this issue given that the market for NBCR terrorism coverage has generally not improved.

CONCLUSION

The TRIA program has worked extremely well over the past ten years -- albeit with no ultimate test on losses and claims -- by providing access for commercial policyholders to insurance against terrorism risk. It has done so through a meaningful public-private partnership that requires and arguably maximizes private sector involvement and unquestionably protects taxpayers in the event of any future act of terrorism. Fortunately, we have yet to see this pay-out and recoupment mechanism in practice, but it nevertheless remains clear that our economic recovery from any such event depends upon having such a plan in place. The terrorism peril is simply too intrinsically linked to government policy and intelligence to be solely handled by the private sector. We therefore commend this Subcommittee for its continued consideration of this important issue, and we urge you to consider a permanent solution that would extend beyond TRIA's current expiration date in 2014. Our CIAT coalition looks forward to working with the Subcommittee on reauthorization.

Thank you again for the opportunity to testify here today, and I am pleased to respond to any questions you may have.

In: Terrorism Risk Insurance
Editor: Oscar A. Madsen

ISBN: 978-1-62618-697-2
© 2013 Nova Science Publishers, Inc.

Chapter 5

TESTIMONY OF ERWANN O. MICHEL-KERJAN, PROFESSOR, WHARTON SCHOOL OF BUSINESS, UNIVERSITY OF PENNSLYVANIA. HEARING ON "TRIA AT TEN YEARS: THE FUTURE OF THE TERRORISM RISK INSURANCE PROGRAM"[*]

Chairman Biggert, Ranking Member Gutierrez, distinguished members of the Subcommittee on Insurance, Housing and Community Opportunity, thank you for inviting me to testify today on "TRIA at Ten Years: The Future of the Terrorism Risk Insurance Program." My name is Erwann Michel-Kerjan. I teach at the Wharton School of the University of Pennsylvania and I am Managing Director of the Wharton Risk Management and Decision Processes Center.

For nearly three decades, the Wharton Risk Center has been at the forefront of basic and applied research to promote effective corporate and public policies for low-probability events with potentially catastrophic consequences (i.e., extreme events) based on an understanding of the decision processes of consumers, firms and public sector agencies.

Since 2008 I have also served as chairman of the OECD Board on Financial Management of Catastrophes, established by Secretary-General

---

[*] This is an edited, reformatted and augmented version of a Testimony Presented September 11, 2012 before the House Committee on Financial Services, Subcommittee on Insurance, Housing and Community Opportunity.

Angel Gurría to advance knowledge on these issues and collaborate closely with the governments and the private sector of the now 34 member countries (including the United States).

The question of how best to manage and finance catastrophes is now high on the agenda of top decision makers around the world given the series of unprecedented disasters and crises that have occurred since 2001. Among all countries, the United States has faced the largest number of untoward events of many different kinds in this short period of time: starting with the 9/11 terrorist attacks, followed by the anthrax attacks, then several major corporate scandals, the Columbia Shuttle accident, followed by the massive blackout, the BP oil spill in the Gulf, the 2004/2005 hurricane seasons (and other significant natural disasters in the ensuing years), and of course the financial crisis from which our economy has yet to fully recover.

America has proved to be a resilient nation. But if this series of events are predictive of what the near future will look like, we as a country have to start a serious discussion about our ability to better prepare for and recover from future catastrophes physically and financially. My Wharton colleague Howard Kunreuther and I made this point explicitly when we jointly testified before the U.S. Senate last year.[1]

Thanks to the leadership provided by Congress, this Subcommittee and especially by you, Chairman Biggert and Congresswoman Maxine Waters, the long overdue reform of the National Flood Insurance Program was passed by Congress at the end of June and signed by the President in early July of this year. This bi-partisan reform was the outcome of over two years of hard work, hearings, and public debates. The Biggert-Waters Flood Insurance Reform Act of 2012 is also based on sound evidence from empirical research produced by leading institutions across the country, including our own team at the Wharton Risk Center.[2]

For those reasons, I want to express my deep respect and gratitude for the extraordinary service you have provided to this nation.[3] Your leadership in reopening the national debate about the future of terrorism risk insurance now, more than two years before the expiration of the temporary Terrorism Risk Insurance Program (TRIP) on December 31, 2014, is very much needed. Today we remember all the victims of the 9/11 tragedy and share our support with their families.

My testimony today will focus on three questions:

1. How has the terrorism risk-sharing between the federal government, the private (re)insurance industry (supply side) and exposed

businesses (demand side) changed with 9/11 and the passage of TRIA 10 years ago? Our team at the Wharton Risk Center has been conducting research on this topic continuously since 2001 so my response to this question will be based on empirical evidence (take up rates, pricing, effects of government intervention).

2. How does a world without TRIA look post 2014? Here, it is critical to imagine the economic consequences of a future attack on U.S. soil. Because we cannot predict when such a catastrophe will occur (if ever again) it is difficult for us to fully evaluate the effectiveness of any program to finance low-probability extreme-impact events. Paradoxically, if the recent increases in federal disaster relief and bailouts serve as evidence, a world without TRIA does not necessarily mean less financial exposure of the federal government to the economic consequences of terrorism. It might very well mean, *de facto*, increased financial liability for all of us as American taxpayers. I will explain why.

3. Finally, how have other OECD countries addressed the terrorism risk coverage challenge? I will briefly highlight the different solutions currently in place in five other countries that have suffered from terrorist attacks on their soil: Israel, Spain, France, the U.K. and Germany. This will build on ongoing work undertaken by the OECD Board I have the honor of chairing and in partnership with the heads of all terrorism risk insurance programs around the world.

I. TERRORISM RISK-SHARING IN THE U.S. FROM 2001 TO TODAY

Terror Insurance Markets Before and Immediately After 9/11

It is important to remind ourselves of the context in which TRIA was established. Before 9/11, major insurance losses from terrorism were viewed as so improbable that the risk was not explicitly mentioned in standard policies (outside of transportation insurance) and hence the cost for providing such coverage to firms was never calculated. Terrorism was covered *de facto* in most commercial insurance contracts.[4] One of the first attacks to significantly impact the insurance industry occurred in the U.K. in 1992 and cost insurers nearly $700 million (indexed to 2001). Then in 1993, three other major

terrorist attacks occurred. The first was the bombing of the World Trade
Center in New York City in February 1993, perpetrated in one of the garages
of the Towers. The bombing killed six people and injured one thousand, and
caused $725 million in insured damages. The second was a series of 13 bomb
attacks in India that killed 300 and injured 1,100 others. Given the lack of
insurance coverage there, these attacks had no major impact on insurers,
though. The third major attack occurred with a bomb exploding near NatWest
Tower in April 1993 in London. This attack triggered $900 million in insured
losses.

Notably, the British insurers recognized the significance of these earlier
attacks for the future of their industry and created a dedicated terrorism
insurance program that same year, Pool Re. Surprisingly, insurers in the U.S. –
and those international insurers and reinsurers covering activities in the U.S. –
continued to cover this peril without explicitly pricing it in their commercial
insurance policies. Two years later, the Oklahoma City bombing killed 168
people, but the largest losses were to federal property and employees, and
were covered by the government. In 1998, bomb attacks on the U.S. embassy
complex in Nairobi, Kenya killed more than 250 people and injured 5,000
others. Still, U.S. insurers and international reinsurers operating here
continued to cover terrorism.

As Berkshire Chairman Warren Buffett said in his November 9, 2001
letter to shareholders:

> "We did not price for manmade mega-cats, and we were foolish in
> not doing so. In effect, we, and the rest of the industry, included coverage
> for terrorist acts in policies covering other risks-and received no
> additional premium for doing so. That was a huge mistake" [5]

Things radically changed on September 11, 2001. The Al Qaeda attacks
killed more than 3,000 people from over 90 countries and injured more than
2250 others (victims of the attacks in New York City, Washington, DC, and
aboard Flight 93 which crashed in Stony Creek Township, Pennsylvania, as
well as among teams of those providing emergency service). The attacks also
inflicted damage estimated at nearly $80 billion, about $32.5 billion (2001
prices, or $42 billion in today's prices) of which was covered by nearly 150
insurers and reinsurers worldwide, many of them in Europe (including $21
billion for damage and business interruption alone).[6] This illustrates the power
of international diversification of these markets.

Private reinsurers, who covered the large portion of these losses, then decided to exit the U.S. market, which they could do, as they are unregulated vis-a-vis the risks they decide to cover. Insurers were thus left without protection for future terrorism catastrophes. By early 2002, insurers had excluded terrorism from their policies in 45 states.[7] Commercial enterprises thus found themselves in a very difficult situation, with insurance capacity extremely limited and, when offered, very highly priced.

September 11, 2002

One year after 9/11, when national security had become the number one priority on the agenda of the United States and other countries, our commercial enterprises remained largely uninsured at home. If another large-scale attack had occurred, the impact on the economy could have been much more serious than it was on 9/11. Indeed, the economic losses would not have been spread over a large number of insurers and reinsurers worldwide. In the absence of massive post-disaster federal relief, these direct and indirect losses such as business interruption, would have been sustained by the firms themselves.

Terrorism Insurance under the Current Public–Private TRIA Arrangement

The lack of availability of terrorism insurance shortly after the 9/11 attacks led to a call from some private sector groups for federal intervention. For example, the U.S. Government Accountability Office reported in 2002 that the construction and real estate industries complained that the lack of available terrorism coverage delayed or prevented several projects from going forward because of concerns by lenders or investors.

In response to such concerns, the Terrorism Risk Insurance Act of 2002 (TRIA) was passed by Congress and signed into law by President Bush on November 26, 2002.[8] This program was originally aimed at providing a three-year temporary measure to increase the availability of risk coverage, but the program has been renewed twice since, in 2005 and 2007. TRIA is now extended up to the end of 2014.

This Subcommittee is familiar with the current design of TRIA so I will not discuss it in detail here. In brief, TRIA requires insurers to offer terrorism coverage to all their commercial clients (a legal "make available" requirement). (Note that residential coverage is not included in this program). These firms have the right to refuse this coverage unless it is mandated by state law, as in the case of workers' compensation in most states.

Loss sharing under TRIA is organized as follows: The first layer is provided by insurers through a deductible. That deductible is calculated as a percentage of the direct earned premiums each insurer received in the preceding year from its policyholders for all lines of business covered under TRIA. In order to increase the role of the private market over time, this percentage has increased sharply from 7% in 2003, to 10% in 2004, 15% in 2005, and it has been 20% since 2007. For some insurers this represents billions of dollars before they receive any federal assistance. The second layer up to $100 billion is the joint responsibility of the federal government and insurers. Specifically, the federal government is responsible for paying 85% of each insurer's primary losses during a given year above the applicable insurer deductible; the insurer covers the remaining 15%.

Contrary to what is done in other countries (see the review in Section III), the U.S. federal government does not collect any premiums for covering 85% of the insurer's losses above the deductible. In essence, the government intervened to provide insurers with free up-front reinsurance for exposure that would ordinarily require a substantial amount of (costly) capital should the insurers seek protection from the private reinsurance market. The "up front" is important here since the U.S. Treasury can recoup part of its payment from insurers over time, in charge for them to recoup this amount against their own policyholders (whether they have suffered from the attack or not, which poses equity issues that have not been discussed at any length in analyses of TRIA).

Has TRIA Worked as Intended?

The main policy goal of TRIA was to ensure that commercial firms across the nation could access subsidized coverage, and as a result, more companies should purchase this coverage.

Market Penetration Has Increased Substantially. The empirical evidence reveals that this strategy has worked. Market data from the two largest insurance brokers, Aon and Marsh, on their own clients (which tend to be larger firms), indicate that commercial take-up rates for terrorism insurance have more than doubled from 27% in 2003 to 60% in 2006, a level that has remained stable since (62% today). These figures have been cited in a number of publications and by my fellow panelists today.

Three important points should be noted about this 60% figure. First, this is not a TRIA take-up rate but combines *all* types of terrorism coverage used by businesses in the United States: U.S. risks only (TRIA only), U.S. risks and non-U.S. risks (clients with foreign values; referred as "TRIA and non-certified"), high risks not covered by the market (referred to as "standalone coverage"), and programs structured as a combination of standalone and TRIA coverage (often done through a captive). Second, these are based on the portfolio of clients of the above two brokers (in other words, these are samples only, not the full market). Third, there is a lot of heterogeneity across industries (e.g., the take-up rate for financial institutions and real estate is around 80% but only 40% in the energy sector).

While we should certainly feel good about the increase observed in 2003-2006, nevertheless, probably about 4 out of 10 large corporations in the United States don't have coverage against terrorism today. Whether they will be able to sustain a large loss with internal or external capital is an open question Congress might want to analyze further. We need to better understand the demand side of this market. Let's remember that on 9/11 the coverage was virtually 100%.

Decrease in Insurance Cost. The increase in coverage is partly due to the fact that terrorism insurance prices have continuously decreased since 2003. The median premium rate for terrorism insurance for middle-size and large firms was down from $57 per million of total insured value (0.0057%) in 2004, $42 per million (0.0042%) to $37 per million (0.0037%) in 2008, then to $25 per million (0.0025%) in 2009 (data from Marsh). A recent report by Aon provides similar information on take-up rates for the twelve months ending March 2012: $20 per million for TRIA coverage only (which translates into an average of about 3.5% of the premium charged for property coverage for TRIA only and about 5% for TRIA and non-certified).[9] This decrease is largely explained by the absence of any new attack on U.S. soil, thanks to the hard work of our government services here and abroad. It is also explained by the natural effect of competition in insurance markets.

Effects of the Federal Intervention. The design of TRIA had another effect on the insurance supply. My colleague Paul Raschky and I recently performed an economic analysis to evaluate how the supply of an additional unit of coverage differed between terrorism insurance (with government intervention) and property insurance (without it). Partnering with Marsh, we were able to undertake a full demand-supply analysis by accessing data on contracts for hundreds of their clients supplied by twenty-six large insurance companies operating in the United States. We find evidence that insurers in the U.S. are much less diversified for terrorism coverage than they are for property lines of coverage, and to some extend for other types of catastrophe risks (e.g., wind and flood); meaning that they would more easily provide additional coverage to a client for terrorism risk than for these other risks.[10]

This result can be interpreted in two ways. On the one hand, and as some have argued, there could be gaming here (*President's Working Group on Financial Markets, Market Conditions for Terrorism Risk Insurance, 2010*): some insurers might be taking on much more terrorism risk with the current free upfront reinsurance from the federal government than they would otherwise, knowing that under TRIA they collect all the terrorism insurance premiums but are responsible for only a portion of the loss. On the other hand, this also means that insurers have provided much more capacity to this market that they would have done otherwise, which was the intent when TRIA was designed.

II. A PARADOX: WHY STOPPING TRIA MIGHT NOT NECESSARILY LOWER THE FEDERAL GOVERNMENT'S EXPOSURE TO FUTURE TERRORISM ECONOMIC LOSSES

TRIA is set to expire at the end of 2014. The question in front of us now is, what do we do next?

- Do we extend TRIA for another few years as is?
- Do we let it expire?
- Do we work to make TRIA more effective and equitable in a redesigned risk-sharing arrangement?

Most of the discussions about TRIA before the 2005 and 2007 renewals have been about whether or not to extend the program. This is likely to be a focal point again in the coming months. At the center of the debate is an argument that can be summarized as follows: if the federal government continues its pattern of renewing TRIA, this will continue to distort the market by displacing long-term private market activity that would have otherwise emerged. It is of course impossible to verify this logic unless one lets TRIA expire and then observe what happens over time, which can be a risky proposition for the federal government as I will show.

Indeed, if the goal behind terminating TRIA is to limit (or avoid any) additional financial exposure of the federal government given the already historical government deficit of $16 trillion today, then terminating TRIA would seem to make sense. The unnoticed paradox, however, is that a world without TRIA (that is, with no federal backstop *and* no mandatory offer requirement) might not necessarily be one with less risk to the federal government and the American taxpayers.

If TRIA expires, and unless reinsurers reentered the U.S. market with much more capacity than they provide today and at a price considered reasonable by insurers, most primary carriers are going to exclude this risk from their portfolio everywhere they can. Those that provide it will charge much higher premiums than they currently do to take into account expensive capital they need to set aside to meet regulatory and/or rating agencies' requirements. As we have seen with the homeowners' hurricane risk insurance market in Florida after the 2004 and 2005 hurricane seasons, new poorly capitalized companies will emerge to take advantage of this situation and write terrorism coverage with a high degree of concentration.

What happens next depends on whether or not another large-scale attack is perpetrated on U.S. soil. If there are no future attacks, the new system will look good (as any would in the absence of claims). But the day after a large attack, we will realize that many firms are uninsured or poorly insured.

Under extreme pressure from the media and interest groups, the federal government will be asked to step in. Only a small portion of the losses will be paid by insurers and their reinsurers, and the large majority of it by all of us as taxpayers. This outcome is pretty certain as one looks at how much more involved the federal government has been in providing financial support after catastrophes and crises in the past decade than it used to be 50 or 60 years ago. If the attack occurs during an election year, this would be even more certain.

Overall, the number of Presidential disaster declarations has dramatically increased over time, from 191 declarations over the decade 1961-1970 to 597 for the period 2001-2010. As Figure 1 also reveals, many of the peak years correspond to presidential election years. In 1996 and 2008 (both presidential election years) there were 75 presidential declarations. This record number was exceeded in 2010 when there were 81 major disaster declarations, and again in 2011 with 99 declarations. Evidence also shows that the portion of economic losses paid by the federal government has been increasing steadily with recent disasters. Maybe we should rethink options before us as to what should be done post 2014, specifically on working to make TRIA more effective and equitable in a redesigned risk-sharing arrangement.

III. HOW HAVE OTHER OECD COUNTRIES ADDRESSED THE TERRORISM RISK COVERAGE CHALLENGE? [11]

In this last section of my testimony I would like to provide some international perspective. This is important for three reasons: a) terrorism threat is international by nature; b) other countries are facing similar challenges as we are as to who should bear the risk of terrorism and how best use the strengths of the private and public sector in developing a robust compensation scheme; and c) in today's global business environment, a growing number of American corporations generate a significant part (if not the majority) of their revenues outside the United States.

I will briefly highlight the solutions currently in place in five other countries that have suffered from terrorist attacks on their soil: Israel, Spain, France, the U.K. and Germany (chronologically, as they developed their program). The material presented below is public information.

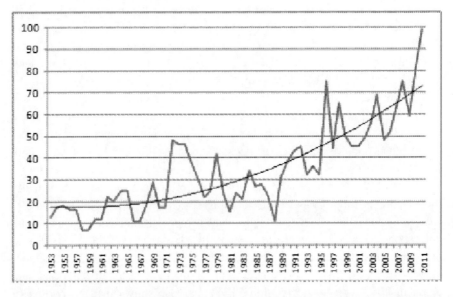

Figure 1. U.S. Disaster Presidential Declarations Per Year, 1953-2011 (data from FEMA).

Israel: Government Coverage, No Involvement of Private Insurers

In this country with a long history of terrorist attacks, losses from attacks are compensated directly by the State according to a pre-defined formula. Any direct and indirect damage occurring within Israel due to war or hostilities will be covered by a *public compensation fund* legislated in 1961. The fund is built from the general property tax collected across the country, according to regulations.

Insurers do not cover this risk. Both individual and business compensation is provided to those who suffer from an attack.

Businesses can also receive claims payments for workers' compensation and loss of business revenues.

Spain: Government Coverage Sold by Private Insurers in its Behalf

Eligibility. Terrorism has been covered as part of the State-backed insurance compensation scheme for extraordinary risks (including also storms, floods, earthquakes, riots), *Consortio de Compensation de Seguros* fund, established in 1954. Coverage for these risks is included as an add-on to property insurance sold by private insurers who are not financially responsible for losses.

The private sector has never expressed an interest in covering terrorism or these other extreme events.

Pricing. Commercial enterprises pay 0.21 euros per thousand of property coverage and another 0.25 euros for business interruption to benefit from this state insurance against extraordinary risks.

Loss History. In the aftermath of the March 11, 2004 terrorist attacks in Madrid, the Consortio paid 41 million euros in claims (railway vehicles were not insured).

The December 2006 attacks against the Barajas Airport triggered another 46 million euros in claims.

These claims were rapidly paid by the Spanish catastrophe fund which currently has over 4 billion euros in reserve and has never used the state guarantee in over 50 years of operation.

France: Public-Private Risk Sharing; Unlimited Government Reinsurance

From a legal perspective, the situation in France was especially acute in the aftermath of 9/11 because the 1986 law does not allow commercial property insurers to dissociate terrorism coverage from commercial property. To stop covering terrorism meant to stop covering commercial property at the 2002 renewals.

The *GAREAT*, a public-private partnership, was established in December 2001 as a co-reinsurance pool organized under a tier structure of risk sharing and shareholders. It operates on an aggregate annual excess of loss basis.

Risk-Sharing Arrangement. The first layer presents an annual aggregate capacity of 400 million euros shared among all 105 members of the pool prorated to their share of ceded business. A second layer is provided by private insurers and reinsurers up to 2 billion euros. Above that, the State layer is an *unlimited* guarantee by the French government provided through the Caisse Centrale de Reassurance (CCR), a state-owned reinsurance company.

Premium Sharing. The premiums levied by insurers against policyholders are transferred to the GAREAT and shared as follows: members of the pool keep nearly 52%, the reinsurance layers 36%, and the CCR receives around 12% of the total annual premiums collected.

Eligibility. Terrorism insurance is mandatory in France, so the take up rate in 100%. The pool covers a large range of French commercial and industrial risks above 20 million euros for property damage and business interruption, including chemical, biological, radiological and nuclear (CBRN) attacks (GAREAT does not cover liability risks and personal lines). Moreover, the same deductible is applied for terrorism as for other property coverage risk pricing.

Pricing. Reinsurance rates by the GAREAT do not vary with location: they are identical across the country. They apply as a percentage of the property premiums and depend only on the total insured value, for which five segments are defined: free (for sums insured below 6 million euros); 6% of the property insurance premium (for sum insured between 6 and 20 million); 12% (between 20 and 50 million euros); 18% (sums insured higher than 50 million euros). Finally, for "special risks" (e.g., nuclear plants) the rate is 24%. This cost is much higher than those I have described for the United States, which are in the 3-to8% range of the property insurance premium.

Renewal and Government Exit Strategy. The pool was first set up for a single year with the option of being renewed, as was done in 2003 until

December 31, 2012. An agreement has been reached recently to renew it on January 1, 2013 for another 5 years.

U.K: Public-Private Risk Sharing; Unlimited Government Debt Issuance

In the wake of the terrorist bomb explosions in London in April 1992, which cost insurers nearly $700 million, and an announcement seven months later by British insurers that they would exclude terrorism coverage from their commercial policies, the U.K. established a mutual reinsurance organization, Pool Re, in 1993 for commercial property and business interruption to accommodate claims resulting from acts of terrorism.

Eligibility. The scale of 9/11 attacks in the United States led to a major revamping of Pool Re. Since the end of 2002, protection of companies operating in the U.K. under Pool Re has been extended to all risks, a category that now includes damage caused by chemical and biological as well as nuclear contamination (while war and related perils as well as computer hacking continue to be excluded).

Risk-Sharing Arrangement. Pool Re acts as a reinsurer for all insurers that wish to be a member of the pool; the U.K. Treasury in turn provides Pool Re with unlimited debt issuance that the pool will have to reimburse over time. Pool Re's right to draw funds under the retrocession agreement with the government is determined on a strict cash needs basis. That means that premium income earned by Pool Re during the time necessary for claims settlement, (i.e. after a terrorist attack), will also be used to pay these claims, if necessary.

All insurers authorized to insure losses arising from damage to commercial property in Great Britain are eligible to apply for membership of Pool Re, regardless of their domicile. Most insurers operating in the U.K. commercial property market are members. As of September 2012, Pool Re has 230 members (75 insurers incorporated in the U.K., 41 Lloyd's syndicates, and 114 insurers incorporated elsewhere). They have an individual retention before being reimbursed by the pool which is based on their proportion of participation in Pool Re, applied to the "industry retention" (£100 million per event, £200 million per year in 2012).

Pool Re has a current reserve of nearly £4.7 billion, which would have to be exhausted before the British Treasury pays anything. If the government needs to intervene for insured losses above this, it will get reimbursed for that payment by the pool over time; and at the end of the day, the members of Pool Re will have paid *all* insured losses due to the terrorist attack.

Premium Sharing. Pool Re shares 10% of its collected premiums with the U.K. government in order to receive this coverage.

Germany: Public-Private Risk Sharing; Limited Government Reinsurance

As in the United States, until the events of 9/11, coverage against terrorism risk was included in all commercial lines in Germany without an explicit extra premium. After 9/11, the extremely limited availability of terrorism coverage led to the founding of *Extremus AG*, a federal government-backed property insurance corporation that started operations on November 1, 2002. Unlike Pool Re, Extremus is not a reinsurance institution but a private insurance company.

Risk-Sharing Arrangement. The annual capacity to pay for claims is 10 billion euros. It is completely reinsured by national and international insurance and reinsurance companies (first layer limited to a total of 2 billion euros), as well as by the federal government (second layer of 8 billion euros). As of December 31, 2010, Extremus provided a total of 450 billion euros terrorism insurance coverage to 1,174 firms.

Premium Sharing. As is the case in France and the U.K., but not in the U.S., the reinsurance provided to Extremus by the federal government is not free of charge: the government receives approximately 12.5% of the 50 million euros in premiums collected by Extremus.

Eligibility. Extremus provides coverage for buildings, contents, and business interruption. But only risks with total insured value over 25 million euros are eligible for coverage. As in the U.S. and the U.K., companies operating in Germany are not required to purchase insurance against terrorism. The annual compensation by Extremus for any company is capped at a maximum of 1.5 billion euros. This means that a company with a total insured value of 25 billion euros it can purchase coverage for only 6% of its total insured value from Extremus. A number of risks are explicitly excluded, such as nuclear risks as well as biological and chemical contamination by terrorists, war and civil war, and insurrection. Losses due to computer viruses are also not covered.

This international review shows that different countries have responded to the question of terrorism risk financing differently, and that those responses were often modified after terrorist attacks on national soil. Some of these concepts may be relevant for the United States as we rethink the role that TRIA should play in the future.

For different governments to be able to compare notes, market developments and ongoing national debate about the future of terrorism risk insurance is important as well. The OECD has taken the lead in making this happen by organizing an unprecedented gathering of all the heads of terrorism risk insurance programs of member countries at its headquarters in Paris in 2010 along with representatives from the private sector and intelligence community;[12] the next meeting of this group will take place on December 4, 2012.

CONCLUSION

The threat of terrorism is still present in the United States even though there has been no successful attack on U.S. soil since 2001. TRIA provides federal reinsurance to insurers at no up-front cost which is unique worldwide. As a result, millions of businesses operating in the United States are able to purchase coverage at a price they judged reasonable. Despite its successes, TRIA can be criticized on several fronts and can certainly be improved. For example, a significant number of firms do not purchase that coverage.

Can the market operate in the absence of a federal backstop and a mandatory offer requirement? Yes, but there is likely to be a rather thin market except for lines that insurers cannot exclude (such as workers' compensation). Could this be sustainable? If there is no successful terrorist act on U.S. soil in the next 10 or 20 years, then yes. But when the next attack occurs, experience shows that Congress will be called to the rescue by businesses that went uninsured, as it has been so many times in recent years for other types of catastrophes and crises.

Instead, I believe we should try to work together at improving the current system, rather than relying on ad hoc response that will come at a time of great sadness and grief. As I showed early in my testimony, an improved TRIA could actually limit the financial liability of the American taxpayers, not increase it.

To make this happen will require leadership from Congress and the Office of the President. As we have done since 2001, my colleagues at the Wharton School and I look forward to working with both on how we do it.

I want to thank you again for the opportunity to testify here today. I would be happy to answer any questions you may have.

End Notes

[1] Kunreuther, H. and E. Michel-Kerjan. Congressional Testimony before the Senate Appropriations Subcommittee on Financial Services and General Government on Federal Disaster Assistance Budgeting: Are We Weather-Ready?, July 28, 2011.
[2] Recent studies include:
 - Michel-Kerjan, E. (2010). Catastrophe Economics: The U.S. National Flood Insurance Program. Journal of Economic Perspectives 24(4): 165–86.
 - Michel-Kerjan, E. and C. Kousky, (2010). Come Rain or Shine: Evidence from Flood Insurance Purchases in Florida, Journal of Risk and Insurance, 77, 369-397 (2010).
 - Michel-Kerjan, E., S. Lemoyne de Forges and H. Kunreuther (2012). Policy Tenure under the U.S. National Flood Insurance Program. Risk Analysis, 32(4): 644-658.
 - Michel-Kerjan, E. and H. Kunreuther (2011). Reforming Flood Insurance. Science 333, July 22.
 - Czajkowski, J., H. Kunreuther and E. Michel-Kerjan (2012). A Methodological Approach for Pricing Flood Insurance and Evaluating Loss Reduction Measures: Application to Texas. Center for Risk Management, The Wharton School, Philadelphia, PA.
[3] Michel-Kerjan, E. and H. Kunreuther. Why We Should Not (Always) Blame Congress. The Huffington Post, August 8, 2012.
[4] Kunreuther, H. and E. Michel-Kerjan. Policy Watch. Challenges of Terrorism Risk Insurance in the U.S. Journal of Economic Perspectives, 2004.
[5] Mr. Buffet's letter is available at: http://berkshirehathaway.com/qtrly_/web1101.html
[6] U.S. Department of the Treasury, Board of Governors of the Federal Reserve System, U.S. Securities and Exchange Commission, Commodity Futures Trading Commission 2006. Terrorism Risk Insurance: Report of the President's Working Group on Financial Markets. Washington, D.C., September.
[7] Large-scale terrorism is different than many other risks: difficulty to quantify the risk, thus to price it actuarially; dynamic nature of the threat, which partly depends on government actions; interdependencies (the vulnerability of one organization depends not only of its own actions but also on actions of other agents) asymmetry of information in favor of government services; potential for catastrophe losses, which would require a lot of costly capital for insurers to cover alone; potential for bankruptcy; and the fact that other risks present a more attractive return on investment insurers can then present their shareholders. See Wharton Risk Center (2005). TRIA and Beyond. The Future of Terrorism Risk Insurance in the U.S. Philadelphia, PA and Kunreuther, H. and E. Michel-Kerjan. Terrorism Insurance 2005. Regulation. The Cato Institute.
[8] The complete version of the original Act can be downloaded at: http://www.treas.gov/offices/domestic-finance/financialinstitution/terrorism-insurance/claims_process/program.shtml.
[9] Aon. Property Terrorism Marketplace. Terrorism Insurance Update. March 15, 2012.
[10] Michel-Kerjan, E. and P. Raschky. The Effects of Government Intervention on the Market for Corporate Terrorism Insurance. European Journal of Political Economy, 2011.

[11] I would like to thank the chairmen, secretary-generals and general managers of the programs discussed here for ongoing discussions and their insights. For more on international terrorism risk insurance markets, see:
- Michel-Kerjan, E. and B. Pedell. (2006). How Does the Corporate World Cope with Mega-Terrorism? Puzzling Evidence from Terrorism Insurance Markets. Journal of Applied Corporate Finance, 18(4):61-75.
- OECD. Terrorism Insurance in OECD Countries, 2005;
- OECD. Terrorism Insurance in 2010: Where Do We Stand? Proceedings of the June 2010 conference, Paris;
- Guy Carpenter. Terrorism. 2011.

[12] Michel-Kerjan, E. Ensuring that Our Economies Remain Terror-Proof. The Huffington Post, June 23, 2010.

In: Terrorism Risk Insurance   ISBN: 978-1-62618-697-2
Editor: Oscar A. Madsen   © 2013 Nova Science Publishers, Inc.

Chapter 6

TESTIMONY OF JANICE OCHENKOWSKI, MANAGING DIRECTOR, JONES LANG LASALLE. HEARING ON "TRIA AT TEN YEARS: THE FUTURE OF THE TERRORISM RISK INSURANCE PROGRAM"[*]

Good morning, Madame Chair Biggert and Ranking Member Gutierrez and members of the Subcommittees. My name is Janice Ochenkowski. I am a Managing Director with responsibility for global risk management for Jones Lang LaSalle, a global real estate and financial services company based in Chicago. I am pleased to be here this morning to testify on behalf of the Risk and Insurance Management Society, Inc. (RIMS). I also appreciate the Subcommittee's foresight and initiative to begin this very important policy debate regarding the reauthorization of the Terrorism Risk Insurance Act on the anniversary of September 11.

RIMS is a not-for-profit organization dedicated to advancing the theory and practice of risk management for the benefit of our member organizations. Our discipline is vital to the creation and protection of physical, financial, and human resources. A global organization and the largest organization of risk managers in the United States, RIMS is comprised of over 10,000 individuals from more than 3,500 entities. 81% of our members are Fortune 500 companies with approximately 1,000 members representing small businesses

---

[*] This is an edited, reformatted and augmented version of a testimony presented September 11, 2012 before the House Committee on Financial Services, Subcommittee on Insurance, Housing and Community Opportunity.

(less than 500 employees). Membership spans the entire economic spectrum from the high-tech sector, real estate, financial, healthcare, energy, transportation and defense. Members also include universities, hospitals, and public entities such as the City of San Francisco, Miami-Dade School District and Orange County, California.

However, as diverse as RIMS member organizations are, they share a common characteristic. That is, they are predominantly large consumers of property and casualty insurance and they have a abiding interest in the need for, and availability of, insurance to cover risk against acts of terror.

APPLICATION OF THE RISK MANAGEMENT DISCIPLINE TO TERRORISM RISK

Risk management is the practice of analyzing an entity's exposures to loss, selecting methods to mitigate the exposures, implementing the selected methods, and monitoring and adjusting the methods depending on the results. Applications for risk management cover all possible exposures to loss, ranging from estimating the number of employees who will be injured in a given period to how to effectively use arbitrage in a global business. The methods used to mitigate exposures are non-insurance transfers, insurance, control, retention, and avoidance. For terrorism exposure, most businesses use a combination of control, retention, and insurance as mitigation strategies.

For example, an owner of real property valued at $10 billion located in the central business districts of major cities, would have a risk management program that would include several different risk management methods to manage concerns about terrorism. Those efforts would include a security program with options such as guards, cameras, motion detectors and alarms, along with an employee and tenant identification program to control building access. Visitors would be limited to one entrance where security staff could log entry and departure. Redundancy and security would be built into all vital computer operations. If the size and potential risk to the property warranted it, the owner might also make physical improvements to the property as well as to the perimeter of the facility. In addition, the owner would purchase an all-risk commercial insurance policy to cover the property for physical damage risks, including terrorism. Property insurance policies have deductibles, and the owner will retain the risk of the deductible amount.

In my job at Jones Lang LaSalle, we purchase insurance for properties owned by our clients through several insurance programs. In total, for U.S. exposures, we purchase insurance for just under 70 million square feet of real estate with an aggregate insured value of under $9 billion. All are commercial properties, and include industrial, retail and residential, but most are office buildings. The locations vary from suburban to city center but are generally within major urban areas in populous states. Since the enactment of the first terrorism legislation, we have been able to purchase terrorism insurance at commercially reasonable limits and in forms acceptable to the properties' lenders. There are some limitations on high risk locations as well as some property types, but in general we are able to buy the coverage we need at premium that can be absorbed by our tenants or investors.

In the event that the Terrorism Risk Insurance Program Reauthorization Act (TRIPRA) is allowed to sunset on December 31, 20014, we believe that we will be unable to obtain the limits of coverage necessary to protect the properties and investors and to satisfy lenders. A more significant portion of the risk will be retained by owners, which would further impede the real estate market's financial recovery. I should also note that tenant leases now frequently require that the landlord maintain terrorism insurance and the inability to purchase the coverage could result in a default on the lease, renegotiation of terms, or loss of a tenant.

One of the basic functions of risk management is to identify potential risks for a company in areas such as property, health and safety, and environmental and financial risk, and to identify options to mitigate those risks. Insurance coverage is a critical and necessary part of the process of protecting our companies from risk, especially risk that can produce catastrophic losses. Terrorism is one of those risks that presents catastrophic exposure to companies. Accordingly, it is vital that terrorism insurance continues to be available to buyers of commercial insurance in a comprehensive and affordable manner when the program expires in 2014.

STABILITY IN INSURANCE MARKETS PROMOTES ECONOMIC STABILITY

RIMS considers the availability of adequate insurance for acts of terrorism to be not simply an insurance problem, but also an economic issue. The inability to acquire sufficient insurance for terrorism coverage could result in the inability to secure financing for future construction projects as well as potential impacts on existing construction projects that require evidence of terrorism coverage.

Without TRIA, many companies would not be able to comply with various lender covenants within mortgages, which would impede the ability to fund real estate transactions and further limit the normal functions of the real estate market.

Additionally, other businesses and public entities face terror exposures critical to the economic well being of our county. Public and private transportation, schools and hospitals, special and sporting events, and certain manufacturing exposures need terrorism coverage as well. Furthermore, as a direct result of 9/11 losses, worker's compensation insurers have restricted coverage for employers with aggregations of workers within a single facility or in large metropolitan areas.

Many businesses and our members in the United States rely on global insurance companies for coverage. These insurers decide where to underwrite risk based on their assessment of overall profitability in return to their shareholders.

If the risk to write coverage is perceived to be too great or uncertain, U.S. businesses will be left without the coverage they need. This could complicate the already fragile economic recovery.

TERRORISM RISK POSES UNIQUE ISSUES OF LOSS PREDICTABILITY

Unpredictability of losses is many times greater for terrorism risk than for natural disasters, as there are no credible historical data on losses. It is impossible to predict frequency with any degree of accuracy, and it is extremely difficult to estimate both the frequency and severity of a potential terrorist event, as the timing, location and target cannot be identified in advance.

Without some form of backstop like TRIA, RIMS believes insurance companies will review their portfolios of business and will refuse to continue covering certain risks in areas where exposure is greatest. This would be true for workers compensation, property, and even third-party liability lines of coverage.

Both large and small businesses would be affected.

CONGRESSIONAL ACTION AND ITS IMPACT ON TERRORISM RISK INSURANCE AVAILABILITY/AFFORDABILITY

The last ten years have demonstrated that the private insurance market alone will likely not be able to respond nor provide adequate coverage for acts of terrorism. Following the events of 9/11 and prior to the passage of TRIA in 2002, the first longterm authorization, the required supply of commercial insurance coverage for acts of terrorism was not available. RIMS members with large concentrations of employees had difficulty in purchasing workers' compensation insurance as well as difficulty in purchasing property insurance coverage, including coverage for terrorism on buildings and construction projects.

Since 9/11, RIMS has conducted a series of intermittent membership surveys (formal and informal) related to member organizations and their access to terrorism risk insurance. In 2006, prior to the passage of TRIPRA, the vast majority of members indicated their policy renewals were conditioned upon Congress' long-term extension of TRIA. As an indicator of what might be expected if a TRIA-type program were not in effect, 75 percent said that prior to the passage of TRIPRA in 2007, their policies contained terrorism coverage conditioned upon the extension of TRIA. Seventy-six percent stated that they believe their terrorism coverage limits would have been decreased had TRIA not been extended, and 82 percent felt their premiums would have increased if TRIA had not been extended. In this regard, one of our members reported that the premiums for coverage of a property in a large metropolitan area went from $200,000 in 2005 to $500,000 in 2006, for one half of the policy limits they had in 2005. Furthermore, the member's broker stated that carriers were unwilling to commit to insuring projects inclusive of TRIA if the completion dates went beyond December 31, 2007, TRIA's original sunset date.

Subsequent to passage of TRIPRA, a 2010 survey of RIMS members indicates that for the most part, capacity is generally not an issue, but continues to be a challenge for risks located in major metropolitan areas, including New York, San Francisco, Chicago, Boston, and Washington, D.C. Based on our members' experience in these densely populated urban areas, the typical situation is that when insurers monitor their aggregate liability in these particular areas, the purchase of adequate insurance can be difficult. Passage of TRIA in 2002 was followed by a demonstrable increase in the number of insurers willing to write the coverage and provide higher limits needed for these high-risk areas. However, this does not hold true for all areas, even today. The amount and cost of coverage available for high-risk locations continues to vary greatly based on the location of the insured and the aggregation of risk in that particular area. If the federal backstop were withdrawn altogether, these urban areas considered high risk, and those more susceptible to terrorist acts and most in need of terrorism risk insurance, would likely be most vulnerable and negatively impacted.

ELEMENTS OF LEGISLATION IN THE 113TH CONGRESS

As to an appropriate Federal role in terrorism reinsurance, RIMS strongly supported bipartisan efforts of this Subcommittee and others to create a Federal Insurance Office (FIO) and worked in coalition to secure its incorporation into the Dodd-Frank Wall Street Reform and Consumer Protection Act.

RIMS support for an FIO was based on the belief in the need for federal coordination on international matters as well as the necessity for a Federal expertise on insurance issues which became apparent in the aftermath of the 9/11 attacks.

As part of this growing recognition that the Federal government has an appropriate role in insurance matters, Congress gave the FIO and Treasury joint authority to administer the Terrorism Insurance Program.

A July 2012 survey of RIMS membership indicates, once again, the strong belief in the necessity of a federal backstop.

Nearly 85% of RIMS respondents indicated that Congress needs to reauthorize TRIPRA and that without another long-term extension, issues of affordability and availability will resurface.

As the Subcommittee and Congress move forward into the next Congress, RIMS supports the following principles in development of another long-term solution:

- A completely private market solution in the long term is probably not feasible because of the difficulty in predicting acts of terrorism and thus being able to price the risk properly. Businesses, as part of their corporate governance, need to be able to assess what the business risks are and how they can be quantified and treated. Without a TRIA-type program, many entities will simply be self-insured due to lack of availability or affordability of coverage or both—leaving their companies and their workers exposed to an event that could bankrupt the company.

- As risk managers, we believe that a program should always be in place to ensure an orderly and efficient response to minimize any market disruptions and ensure benefits are available to any victims—individuals or companies from a catastrophic loss scenario.

- A private/public partnership provides the best alternative to addressing the long-term needs of availability and affordability of insurance to cover acts of terrorism. Some form of risk pooling may be an appropriate approach. Regardless of the extent of private market involvement, the federal government will likely be required to continue to be involved in a reinsurance capacity at some level with the level of involvement decreasing over time.

- The solution needs to address the long-term availability and affordability of insurance coverage for nuclear, biological, chemical, and radiological (NBCR) events caused by terrorism. RIMS believes it is critical that a program be developed to insure continued coverage for acts of terrorism, including nuclear, biological, chemical, and radiological acts. The federal government has stated that potential acts of terrorism from these sources are likely. RIMS believes that NBCR represents some of the most problematic areas in the ongoing terrorism debate. The stand-alone terrorism insurance market continues to be extremely limited, in that it really only exists for the property line and is very limited in terms of capacity and price. Rating agencies are increasing the capital requirements for reinsurers, which means that they cannot write the same limit of coverage as last year without increasing their capital reserves. The practical impact is that available limits of coverage will be reduced. RIMS believes that it is critical that a long-term solution be developed to insure that terrorism insurance will be available.

- All commercial property, workers' compensation, auto and general liability lines should be included in any new plan.

- Insurance companies writing commercial lines should be required to participate in the program and be required to make coverage available for acts of terrorism.

- Tax incentives and eligibility for participation in the program should be considered to encourage creation of private insurance capacity.

RIMS appreciates the opportunity to testify and thanks the Subcommittee for beginning this very important discussion in advance of TRIPRA's expiration.

In: Terrorism Risk Insurance
Editor: Oscar A. Madsen

ISBN: 978-1-62618-697-2
© 2013 Nova Science Publishers, Inc.

Chapter 7

TESTIMONY OF LINDA ST. PETER, OPERATIONS MANAGER, PRUDENTIAL CONNECTICUT REALTY. HEARING ON "TRIA AT TEN YEARS: THE FUTURE OF THE TERRORISM RISK INSURANCE PROGRAM"*

INTRODUCTION

Chairwoman Biggert, Ranking Member Gutierrez, and members of the Subcommittee, on behalf of more than 1.1 million REALTORS®, thank you for inviting me to testify today on the future of the terrorism risk insurance program. My name is Linda St. Peter. I am the 2012 Vice Chair of the Commercial Committee for the National Association of REALTORS® (NAR) and I am the current operations manager for Prudential Connecticut Realty in Wallingford, CT. I have specialized in commercial and investment real estate brokerage, since 1988. I am pleased to testify of behalf of the NAR and its commercial affiliates: CCIM Institute, Institute of Real Estate Management, REALTORS® Land Institute, and Society of Industrial and Office REALTORS®. Together, members of NAR and its affiliates are involved in all

---

* This is an edited, reformatted and augmented version of a Testimony Presented September 11, 2012 before the House Committee on Financial Services, Subcommittee on Insurance, Housing and Community Opportunity.

aspects of commercial real estate – from real estate brokerage to property management.

RECENT ATTACKS & THREATS

We still live in an uncertain world and continue to fight the war on terror. Though we have been safe at home since September 2001, we only need to look to the 2011 suicide bombing at Moscow's Domodevo airport for terrorism's devastating potential. Additionally, conflict in many countries across the Middle East and North Africa has increased political and social tensions, factors that suggest terrorism risk will be a constant and potentially growing threat for years to come. It is in the interest of America's economic security to ensure that as much of our commercial real estate industry is covered by terrorism insurance as possible.

Through my experience working on some of Connecticut's most significant commercial real estate projects over the past several years, I personally understand the vital importance of terrorism insurance to accomplishing the economic goals of Connecticut. I can tell you that if the terrorism insurance program were to expire, many of my firm's community development projects would not be possible.

IMPORTANCE OF TERRORISM INSURANCE

It is no secret that immediately after the horrific 9/11 terrorist attacks, terrorism insurance coverage was virtually non-existent for commercial property owners. Only when Congress enacted the Terrorism Risk Insurance Act (TRIA) in 2002 did coverage for terrorist attacks resume. TRIA established a public-private risk-sharing partnership that allows the federal government and private insurance companies to share losses in the event of a major terrorist attack. Originally enacted as a 3-year program, TRIA has been reauthorized by Congress twice. In 2005, Congress passed the Terrorism Risk Insurance Extension Act (TRIEA). The most recent extension – the Terrorism Risk Insurance Reauthorization Act of 2007 (TRIPRA) – extended the program through December 31, 2014.

Today, there is concern that the uncertain future of TRIA may cause insurance prices to fluctuate. Further, this uncertainty may prompt insurers to drop terrorism coverage if a reauthorization of the program is not in place by the end of 2014. This became evident in 2005 when private insurers became more reluctant to offer terrorism coverage due to uncertainty regarding the program's extension. Ultimately, the uncertainty of insurance pricing impacts our net operating income, and the value of our properties. The potential unavailability of this coverage at the end of 2014 will impact our financing agreements and potentially hurt the fragile commercial real estate market.

Affordable and available terrorism insurance is a vital component of most commercial real estate transactions. It is estimated that 84 percent of outstanding commercial mortgage balances require terrorism insurance. Thus, if TRIA were to expire, and insurers subsequently dropped terrorism coverage, those loans would be in technical default. While the commercial real estate finance market is starting to show signs of life, any disruption in the availability of terrorism insurance in this sector would have serious consequences on its fragile road to recovery.

NECESSITY OF THE TERRORISM RISK INSURANCE PROGRAM

The passage of TRIA in 2002 helped stabilize commercial real estate markets following the disruptions of the September 11, 2001, terrorist attacks by making terrorism coverage available and, over time, more affordable. According to a 2010 President's Working Group on Capital Markets (PWG)[1] and 2008 Government Accountability Office (GAO) study[2], TRIA and its subsequent extensions have generally kept terrorism insurance affordable and available nationwide. Owners of high-value properties in urban areas, such as Manhattan, however, still face challenges in obtaining coverage at a reasonable price. Improved access and lower premiums are due in part to the continued improvement in an insurer's ability to model and measure their aggregate loss exposure, and thereby manage terrorism risk.

However, despite improvements in these measurements, the frequency and severity of terrorism attacks cannot be reliably assessed by insurance companies. Primary insurers remain largely averse to exposing themselves to potentially catastrophic terrorism losses and continue to have limited availability to reinsurance. Reinsurance plays a critical role in insurance markets by allowing insurers to transfer some of the risks they assume in offering, permitting them to offer additional coverage. Similar to the challenges faced by primary insurance companies, reinsurers have limited ability to predict the frequency and magnitude of future terrorist attacks, which has hindered reinsurers from sufficiently managing the industry's current terrorism risk exposure.

Thus, without the federal backstop for potential insurance losses related to terrorism, we believe coverage availability could decline significantly. In fact, without TRIA providing reimbursement for insured losses that exceed the amount of an insurer's deductible, coverage could decline by more than 95 percent, according to one insurance company cited in the GAO report.

RECENT MODIFICATIONS TO TRIA

As mentioned earlier, since its enactment in 2002, TRIA has been modified and extended twice. We believe many of the changes made have enhanced the program by providing more access to affordable terrorism insurance for businesses, while lowering the potential cost to taxpayers in the event of a major terrorist attack.

This includes the removal of the foreign vs. domestic terrorism distinction. Without this change, the Treasury Secretary may be forced to make determinations that may not serve our national security needs, and more importantly, the distinction served no policy goal. As the 2005 London bombing demonstrated all too well, there can be serious difficulties in distinguishing between foreign and domestic terrorism, and the distinction makes no difference to the victims.

PRINCIPLES FOR A LONG TERM SOLUTION

Quite simply, an effective homeland security strategy is central to the nation's economic security. American businesses must have adequate terrorism risk coverage. Without terrorism insurance, the nation's economic infrastructure is totally exposed to large-scale business disruptions after an attack, and to a retarded recovery from the damage that is caused by the attack. As our economic interests continue to be targeted by terrorists, it is appropriate, necessary, and vital that the federal government play a role in maintaining the security of our insurance system which helps provide for recovery of the economy.

Extension & Structure of Program

We believe the time has come for Congress to enact a long-term solution for insuring against terrorism – one that provides the needed market certainty to allow for continued economic growth and development. We envision a two-part structure that would finance both conventional terrorism risks and nuclear, biological, chemical, and radiological (NBCR) risks.

Conventional Terrorism Risk. For risk of conventional (i.e., non-NBCR) terrorism attacks, we believe the current TRIA backstop should be kept in place, with the insurance deductibles, industry retention, and program trigger all maintained at no higher than their current levels. This ensures policyholders will continue to have access to coverage through the "make available" provision.

While TRIA has been largely successful in making available private direct insurance coverage against conventional terrorism attacks, it has not been without some continuing problems of availability and affordability. There are still major markets today, particularly high-risk urban areas, where the combination of aggregation risk, high retention rates, and rating agency pressure are causing capacity problems for conventional terrorism coverage. Therefore, Congress and the federal government need to continue the statutory framework that is known as TRIA for conventional terrorism exposure, but this framework needs to be modernized to reflect the continuing market realities of capacity shortfalls in some areas.

NBCR Terrorism Risk. NBCR terrorism risk is a different matter. Even if the federal backstop exposure to conventional terrorism can be reduced over time to all but the most catastrophic attacks, the challenges are different for NBCR, according to all of the expert actuarial estimates. As it presently stands, TRIA covers NBCR perils; however, we have not seen any evidence that such coverage is being written except when mandated for workers compensation. Because TRIA only requires that terrorism insurance coverage be made available on the same terms, amounts, and limitations as non-terrorism perils, insurers are not required to make NBCR terrorism coverage available if NBCR coverage for non-terror events is not offered.

The GAO and the PWG reports have all recognized that markets simply cannot price the risks associated with NBCR perils. Accordingly, we believe that this is a crucial area that the long-term solution should address. NAR believes NBCR coverage and pricing can be improved if Congress adopts measures that would lower insurer deductibles and co-pays with respect to NBCR risks. It is also necessary for Congress to clarify that the federal government is solely liable for NBCR terrorism losses above insurers' individual NBCR retentions, thus encouraging insurers to provide more capacity. Finally, we urge Congress to add NBCR perils to the "make available" requirement under TRIA so that policyholders would have an optional endorsement giving them coverage for NBCR terrorism that would otherwise be excluded by the nuclear hazard or pollution exclusion contained in certain commercial lines policies.

CONCLUSION

Affordable and accessible terrorism insurance is an integral part of the health of the commercial real estate markets. Given that the reinsurance industry has not yet been able to develop a long-term solution that would eliminate the need for some form of federal assistance, NAR is concerned that the potential sunset of TRIA will result in a spike in terrorism coverage premiums, and cause coverage to become unavailable in numerous markets.

NAR believes the TRIA program has been a success because it provides for the sharing of risk between government, private insurers, and policyholders. Ultimately, it is critical for the U.S. economy that commercial policyholders be able to obtain coverage for terrorism risk. Therefore, TRIA must be extended beyond its current 2014 authorization.

End Notes

[1] Market Conditions for Terrorism Risk Insurance 2010, Report of the President's Working Group on Financial Markets.
[2] GAO, Report to Congressional Committees, Terrorism Insurance – Status of Efforts by Policyholders to Obtain Coverage (GAO-08-1057, Sept. 2008).

In: Terrorism Risk Insurance ISBN: 978-1-62618-697-2
Editor: Oscar A. Madsen © 2013 Nova Science Publishers, Inc.

Chapter 8

STATEMENT OF STEVE BARTLETT, PRESIDENT AND CEO, THE FINANCIAL SERVICES ROUNDTABLE. HEARING ON "TRIA AT TEN YEARS: THE FUTURE OF THE TERRORISM RISK INSURANCE PROGRAM"[*]

Chairwoman Biggert, Ranking Member Gutierrez, and Members of the Subcommittee, thank you for the opportunity to testify today — appropriately and humbly as we meet on September 11th.

I am Steve Bartlett, the President and CEO of the Financial Services Roundtable.

The Roundtable is a national trade association composed of 100 of the nation's largest banking, securities and insurance firms. Our members provide a full range of financial products and services to consumers and businesses. Member companies participate through the Chief Executive Officer and other senior executives nominated by the CEO.

Roundtable member companies provide fuel for America's economic engine, accounting directly for $92.7 trillion in managed assets, $1.2 trillion in revenue, and 2.3 million jobs.

---

[*] This is an edited, reformatted and augmented version of a statement presented September 11, 2012 before the House Committee on Financial Services, Subcommittee on Insurance, Housing and Community Opportunity.

TRIA IS A NEEDED PUBLIC-PRIVATE PARTNERSHIP

The property & casualty insurance sector is an important part of the country's physical and economic infrastructure. Insurance helps protect the U.S. economy from the adverse effects of the risks inherent in economic growth and development. Insurance also provides the resources necessary to rebuild physical and economic infrastructure in the event of catastrophic losses to persons or property. Insurance provides a safety net that is critical to healthy economic activity.

The Financial Services Roundtable supports the Terrorism Risk Insurance Act (TRIA), which provides an absolutely essential federal backstop in the face of catastrophic losses arising from a terrorist attack. Importantly, any federal outlay may, under the statute, be recouped by assessments on policyholders. In addition, it is imperative that the program be reauthorized to avoid disruptions in coverage.

TRIA, and the Terrorism Risk Insurance Program it created, provides stability in the market by making an uninsurable risk insurable. Originally signed into law on November 26, 2002, TRIA was amended by the Terrorism Risk Insurance Extension Act of 2005 and the Terrorism Risk Insurance Program Reauthorization Act of 2007, and is now set to expire on December 31, 2014. TRIA must be reauthorized because it makes terrorism risk insurance accessible. It provides an orderly mechanism through which terrorism losses are absorbed by the private sector, and because it helps support the economy when we as a country are attacked.

TERRORISM RISK PRESENTS UNIQUE CHALLENGES

Effective insurance underwriting requires the ability to predict with some accuracy frequency, location and severity (amount of loss). Though normal insurance risks can be unpredictable, when those events are assessed over a large enough area and timeline, the randomness of those events provide a pattern which informs underwriting decisions and allows insurance companies to cover the appropriate level of risks.

Terrorism changes that equation because it is not random; it is purposeful. Neither the frequency nor severity of the attack can be predicted or modeled. A terrorist may not act for years and then strike multiple times in multiple different ways, none of which is predictable. This dynamic risk, driven by free will and unlimited in scope, makes managing the risk by the private sector near impossible. Terrorism knows no geographic, seasonal, or other objectively verifiable pattern. It can happen anywhere, any time and in any way imagined by the mind of the terrorist.

Modeling methodologies for terrorism are also nascent. While insurers continue to refine modeling methodologies, underwriters have yet to identify a model that can account for the erratic and purposeful behavior of a terrorist. These difficulties are substantially compounded by the very nature of terrorist activity — terrorists seek to disguise intent and their planned actions — and the highly secure nature of government intelligence sources. Similarly, there is no way to predict the severity of an event. Depending on the type of attack, thousands of dollars, millions of dollars or billions of dollars in insured commercial activity can be at risk. Absent TRIA, the insurance industry's ability to absorb another terrorist attack, whether on the magnitude of September 11, 2001, or worse, is compromised. State legislatures and insurance regulators limit the industry's ability to manage or limit terrorism exposure and, since catastrophic terrorism is unpredictable, insurers cannot adequately price the exposure and are subject to a significant degree of adverse selection. TRIA is essential to ensure that the risk spreading mechanism that is the foundation of the insurance industry, works. We acknowledge that even with TRIA, the insurance industry remains vulnerable to significant financial disruption in the event of another catastrophic terrorism attack given the substantial insurer retentions TRIA requires. Similarly, in the absence of an effective backstop for terrorism losses, another terrorist attack, especially if the impact is concentrated on a small group of primary insurers, may very well be enough to render the industry unable to absorb a second catastrophic loss, such as from a hurricane, earthquake or other natural catastrophe.

We have insufficient experience, significant modeling uncertainty, incomplete data, and a huge loss potential that may exceed the insurance industry's claims paying ability. It is, therefore, critical that the U.S. continues to have a backstop for the largest events.

TRIA Is Designed to Keep the Wheels of Commerce Moving

Prior to 9/11, insurance companies included insurance for terrorism risk in their general policies with no additional premium assessed for this risk.

Following that tragic day, insurers were left with little option but to exclude terrorism coverage as an uninsurable risk from policies. There was little or no market for commercial policyholders who sought coverage.

In the absence of all-peril coverage, banks and other investors were less willing to lend or invest money in construction projects and businesses without terrorism coverage; this ultimately hampered construction and jobs. During the fourteen-month period between 9/11 and the passage of TRIA, approximately $15 billion in real estate-related transactions were delayed or cancelled, according to the Real Estate Roundtable. During that same period, the White House Council of Economic Advisors estimated that 300,000 jobs were lost.

TRIA was designed to mitigate the negative economic impact from the stalled real-estate development and investment. First and foremost, TRIA includes a "make available" provision, which means that insurers must offer terrorism insurance to commercial clients. With coverage available, banks looking to lend and investors looking to deploy their capital can do so while protecting their investments from the threat of a terrorist attack.

With TRIA in place, the number of business that purchased terrorism insurance has risen dramatically. In 2003, the take-up rate was 27 percent; by 2009, the take-up rate rose to 61 percent, according to a 2010 Marsh Report.

TRIA ENSURES PRIVATE SECTOR PROTECTION OF TERRORISM RISK

TRIA ensures that private insurance and reinsurance pays the first losses in the event of a terrorist attack. The current version of TRIA has a "program trigger" of $100 million for certified acts of terrorism, under which the private sector takes all the loss. If losses exceed $100 million, each individual insurance company with losses will realize the entire loss up to 20 percent of its direct written premium the prior year — for some companies this would be over $1 billion in money being paid out before one dollar of government money is spent.

Following the 20 percent deductible, private insurers begin to share losses with the federal government; the government absorbs 85percent of additional losses and the private sector absorbs the remaining 15 percent with a program cap of $100 billion.

Importantly, if the government backstop is called upon, the law requires that government payments will be recouped by increasing future policyholders' premiums by up to 3 percent a year. Government funding for events that occur after January 1, 2012, must be collected by September 30, 2017.

FAILURE TO EXTEND TRIA WOULD HAVE ECONOMIC CONSEQUENCES

Without federal support, insurers' limited ability to manage terrorism risk would become unstable and they would withdraw or reduce their offerings. This is neither supposition nor hyperbole — we know how the market reacts in the absence of this program. In the absence of TRIA, limited insurance and reinsurance for terrorism risk will be available, and what is available will be offered at largely cost-prohibitive prices. Lending, especially for large-scale development in high-risk areas will be significantly restricted as credit is not extended to businesses unable to obtain terrorism risk insurance.

According to a 2010 President's Working Group report, marketplace terrorism risk insurance capacity has increased. Nevertheless, capacity is constrained and commercial insurance policyholders have difficulty obtaining coverage with sufficient limits Essentially, market capacity is improving, but it is not sufficient. TRIA requires that terrorism coverage is available and provides the market the tools to grow.

THE ALTERNATIVE TO TRIA IS NO PROTECTION AT ALL

While some have argued TRIA exposes U.S. taxpayers to losses that will increase an already high debt and deficit, the opposite is actually true. As detailed above, losses from a terrorist act must reach a substantial total before the federal government becomes involved by loaning funds to pay claims. And once that level is reached, the insurer shares those losses with the federal government and then uses future premium charges to repay federal funds.

In fact, TRIA puts in a place an orderly system to make sure that the private sector absorbs most if not all of the losses. Without TRIA, terrorism insurance will be available only in limited quantities. This not only deters investments and costs jobs, but it also means that little to no coverage is in place if another attack occurs. It is difficult to imagine a situation in which the federal government will not be forced to absorb the loss from such an attack

— when businesses are left with no protection from physical and financial disaster.

The risk of such an attack is not limited to a geographic region, industry or target. It can happen anywhere. And no matter where it happens, its impact goes far beyond that specific target. High-density areas and high-value properties have more difficulty obtaining coverage, but commerce is interconnected. What happens in one region or to one location has ramifications across the country. If a port or transportation hub is disabled by an attack, businesses that rely on that center in their supply chain are damaged and may face business continuity challenges.

But it is important to remember, the ultimate target of a terrorist attack is likely not a business or particular building. Rather, it is the government and population of the United States. If future attacks do occur, we, as a country, must respond to support our citizens and businesses. TRIA acknowledges this by ensuring that the U.S. response is one that supports its people and its economy by providing a mechanism in which such unpredictable losses can be underwritten and absorbed by the private sector.

CONCLUSION

The Roundtable applauds the Subcommittee for its attention to this topic at such an early date. Although expiration seems a long way off, business decisions that involve terrorism risk coverage are continually being made; if uncertainty is allowed to persist around renewal of the program, we will see an increasingly negative impact on the economy.

The Roundtable strongly believes TRIA should be reauthorized. Doing so will make our economy and country stronger. We look forward to working with you on this important issue. I am happy to answer any questions.

In: Terrorism Risk Insurance
Editor: Oscar A. Madsen

ISBN: 978-1-62618-697-2
© 2013 Nova Science Publishers, Inc.

Chapter 9

STATEMENT OF DARWIN COPEMAN, PRESIDENT AND CHIEF EXECUTIVE OFFICER, JEWELERS MUTUAL INSURANCE COMPANY. HEARING ON "TRIA AT TEN YEARS: THE FUTURE OF THE TERRORISM RISK INSURANCE PROGRAM"[*]

INTRODUCTION

Chairman Biggert, Ranking Member Guiterrez, and members of the House Financial Services Subcommittee on Insurance, Housing and Community Opportunity, thank you for the opportunity to provide testimony on the Terrorism Risk Insurance Act (TRIA) and its vital role in helping protect our country and our economy as we continue to consider how to best handle the threat of terrorism.

My name is Darwin Copeman and I am president and chief executive officer of Jewelers Mutual Insurance Company. A mid-sized company founded in 1913 and headquartered in Neenah, Wisconsin. Jewelers Mutual is licensed in all 50 states and is the only insurance company in the U.S. that specializes exclusively in protecting the jewelry industry and individuals' jewelry. Our company participates in the TRIA program and understands first-

---

[*] This is an edited, reformatted and augmented version of a Presented September 11, 2012 before the House Committee on Financial Services, Subcommittee on Insurance, Housing and Community Opportunity.

hand its importance of this unique partnership between the private insurance industry and the federal government.

Jewelers Mutual is proud to be a member of the National Association of Mutual Insurance Companies (NAMIC) made up of 1,400 property/casualty insurance companies serving more than 135 million auto, home and business policyholders, with more than $196 billion in premiums accounting for 50 percent of the automobile/homeowners market and 31 percent of the commercial insurance market. NAMIC is the largest and most diverse property/casualty trade association in the country, with regional and local mutual insurance companies on main streets across America joining many of the country's largest national insurers who also call NAMIC their home. More than 200,000 people are employed by NAMIC members.

It is our firm belief that the threat of terrorism is not an insurable risk. As such, no self-sustaining private market for terrorism risk coverage is likely to develop. However, the presence of a robust private/public partnership that has provided stability and predictability has allowed insurers to actively participate in the market in a meaningful way. Without a program such as TRIA, many of our citizens who want and need terrorism coverage to operate their businesses all across the nation would be either unable to get insurance or unable to afford the little coverage that would be available. The result when the next terrorist attack occurs, will be more − not less − federal exposure as the government will be under extreme pressure to pay for *all* of the losses.

Therefore, we believe it is vitally important to our nation's finances, security, and economic strength that we maintain a long-term private/public partnership for terrorism risk insurance.

THE NATURE OF TERRORISM RISK

Before the events of September 11, the abstract possibility of a major terrorist attack on the U.S. was known, but largely dismissed by most people. At the time, terrorism was typically included in "all-risk" policies because the risk was deemed so small as to be incalculable. Overnight, the insurance industry's understanding of the nature of terrorism risk fundamentally changed.

What became immediately clear is that managing terrorism risk defies the normal underwriting practices of insurers. First, it was apparent that there was an absence of meaningful actuarial data that insurers normally rely on when considering whether coverage can be offered and, if so, at what price. In the case of natural catastrophe risk for example, a company can rely on decades of relevant event data that can be plugged into mathematical models to quantify risk – there is no comparable historical record on which to draw for large-scale terrorist events. Further, much of the relevant data that might be used by an insurance company is appropriately kept secret by the federal government for national security reasons. Without access to this type of information insurers cannot meaningfully calculate the likelihood, nature, or extent of a potential event, making pricing and reserving virtually impossible.

Second, like the risk from flooding, the risk is too highly concentrated to effectively pool across geographical locations and policyholder type, particularly in an age of mass-casualty terror. Acts of terrorism on the scale of 9/11 are what are known as a "clash events" meaning they cause significant losses across multiple lines of insurance. In the case of the attack on the World Trade Center, there were enormous insured losses in the property, liability, life, and workers compensation lines, among others. Naturally, these types of events directly threaten the solvency of both insurers and reinsurers and are not typically covered risks. In a fully free market, it would likely be the case that highly concentrated urban areas in particular would find it difficult to find or afford coverage for terrorism.

Third, there is no clear way to determine the possible severity of a given attack, particularly those using nuclear, chemical, biological, or radiological (NCBR) weapons. There is no real loss data to rely on to understand the extent of damage from such weapons. That said, several years ago, the Rand Corporation found that "a radiological attack in an urban core would likely lead to catastrophic levels of uninsured business interruption and property losses." The American Academy of Actuaries estimated potential losses from a NCBR attack in New York City at $778 billion, which is more than *three times* the commercial property/casualty industry's claims-paying capacity.[1] These estimates underscore the uninsurability of such an event.

Fourth, the existence of interdependencies in local, national, and global systems further complicates any effort to accurately price terrorism risk insurance. At the very highest level, the nation's foreign policy decisions and the effectiveness of its homeland defense have a direct impact on the likelihood and success of an attack. At the policyholder level, the vulnerability of one organization is not simply dependent on its own security decisions, but also on the decisions of other organizations and agents beyond its control. Further, interdependence does not require geographical proximity – one need only consider the 2001 anthrax scare utilizing the U.S. Postal Service to grasp that breakdowns in systems far away can have a serious impact on potential losses.

Finally, and most importantly, is the human element. The fact that human beings plan and strategically execute terrorist events means that these events are not fortuitous; they are caused deliberately and do not occur randomly. Because of this, there is no way to determine the probability that a particular property or asset will experience a terrorism-related loss. Part of the difficulty in assessing terrorism risk stems from the fact that, because of response measures taken in the wake of an attack, the next event is unlikely to follow a similar pattern. Unlike criminal acts such as robbery where the goals are predictably targeted, the goal of maximizing death and destruction can be accomplished in countless ways, anywhere, and at any time.

All of the above factors lead us to conclude that it is unlikely that insurers will ever have the necessary tools to predict when, where, and how terrorist events will occur. Immediately following 9/11, there was hope that, given time, more accurate modeling could be developed and utilized to help insurers manage this type of risk. And indeed, much has been done to develop tools to manage aggregate loss exposures that are based on a predetermined event of a certain magnitude in a given area. However, models that attempt to predict the frequency or severity of an attack are not considered reliable. Given that modeling is typically effective only in determining the likelihood that particular events will occur and the fact that the data inputs will always be extremely limited, improved modeling will not solve the fundamental challenges of offering terrorism coverage.

Similarly, the nature of terrorism risk does not allow insurers and risk managers to create effective mechanisms to mitigate the risk of loss due to terrorism. Unlike in other types of coverage where a policyholder might get a premium discount for storm-proofing her home, it is not at all clear how a commercial property-owner could reduce the probability of experiencing a terrorism-related loss. With the interdependencies mentioned above the possible scenarios are endless – a company might spend a significant sum of money to secure a facility while a neighboring company does not and is then used as a staging area for an attack. Additionally, the presence of human volition drastically reduces the value of preventative measures, given that a terrorist usually will plan an attack with those measures in mind. Again, terrorism is not comparable to a random event – a hurricane cannot study wind-damage mitigation efforts and then think up new ways to get around them. The only truly effective mitigation tools – if there are any -- reside within the government's national security apparatus, and as noted above, these are understandably kept secret.

No amount of innovation in catastrophe modeling and risk mitigation will change the factors that fundamentally distinguish catastrophic events randomly caused by natural forces, from catastrophic events caused by the calculated machinations of human beings. In any discussion about terrorism risk or the TRIA program, we must be clear about the unique nature of the terrorist threat.

The difficulty facing risk managers who wish to purchase private insurance coverage for terrorism-related events can be seen in the recent experience of the city of Chicago. To manage the liability risk associated with hosting a two-day NATO summit in mid-May, the city sought, and was able to easily acquire from domestic insurers, liability coverage for slip-and-fall accidents, automobile damage, and medical coverage. But city officials also feared that this important international gathering could be the target of a terrorist attack. They therefore attempted to purchase additional coverage for any liability the city might incur specifically related to terrorism. Insurance brokers acting on the city's behalf were unable to find a single standard commercial insurer that was willing to provide the needed coverage at any price. The city was finally able to purchase a policy from Lloyd's of London, which is known for insuring unusual risks. According to a report in the Chicago Tribune, the policy, which provided $100 million in terrorism liability coverage for just two days, cost the city $1.3 million. That premium represented more than 10 percent of the total cost of hosting the NATO summit.

It should be noted that the $100 million liability limit under the city's Lloyd's policy is equal to event "trigger" under TRIA, so that in effect, the TRIA backstop for losses in excess of that amount was irrelevant to this transaction. Yet the city's $100 million policy limit would not even begin to cover the potential property losses from a large-scale terrorist attack launched in downtown Chicago. Based on Chicago's NATO summit experience, it seems reasonable to conclude that in the absence of TRIA, few if any private insurers would be willing to provide the much larger amount of property coverage that would be needed to insure a large office building or hotel. Indeed, Chicago's experience suggests that, if anything, Congress should consider lowering the event trigger when it begins the work of extending the TRIA program beyond its 2014 expiration date. If the current trigger had been set at, say, $50 million, Chicago would probably have found numerous domestic insurers willing to offer the coverage it needed, and at a much lower premium.

The story of Chicago's search for terrorism liability insurance is noteworthy because it forcefully illustrates that the real beneficiaries of TRIA are not insurance companies, but the many entities that need the financial protection from terrorism that can only be provided by terrorism insurance that is both available and affordable. These beneficiaries consist not only of commercial enterprises, but include America's cities and other government entities as well.

THE TRIA PROGRAM

The 9/11 attacks caused roughly $40 billion in insured losses. Soon after the events, reinsurers and insurers moved to exclude terrorism coverage from their new and renewing policies. There were certain at-risk areas of the country that saw extremely hard markets in property and workers compensation coverage. In states like New York which prohibited carriers from excluding coverage for terrorism and with reinsurance companies universally excluding terrorist acts in property/casualty treaties, most carriers' only alternative was to offer less coverage or not write the business at all.

The few companies willing to provide coverage increased their prices because of the significant terrorism exposure. However, many of those companies began to cut back when concentrations of values and employees became too large. Again using New York as an example, the lack of adequate insurance capacity and significant increases in pricing of commercial multi-peril business resulted in the postponement of many construction projects. It was estimated at the time to have delayed or cancelled $15.5[2] billion in real estate transactions and cost 300,000 construction workers their jobs.[3]

Given this economic uncertainty and the insurance industry's uncertainty about its ability to properly manage terrorism risk, Congress passed and President George W. Bush signed into law the Terrorism Risk Insurance Act of 2002. The bill established TRIA as a temporary federal government program that created a private-public partnership to share in the compensation for privately insured commercial property/casualty losses resulting from acts of terrorism. The program was designed to guard against further economic dislocation and to allow the insurance industry a transition period to develop the capacity to adequately provide terrorism insurance without government involvement. At the time, some analysts thought that it might be possible to develop a truly private market for terrorism given time to build capacity and to study the risk. However, it was soon realized – for the reasons discussed above

– that without the program American businesses would be hard pressed to find or afford the coverage they needed and so TRIA was extended for two years in 2005 and again in 2007 for seven years. Both extensions included modifications that required a greater share of the potential losses be borne by the private sector. Essentially, the program is a federal backstop for commercial property/casualty insurance that acts as reinsurance in the event of a certified terrorist event. A private insurance company pays for losses up to a certain level and then the government covers the majority of the losses up to a ceiling of $100 billion, after which neither the government nor the company is required to pay further. The private sector insurers' share of the losses is made up of several components:

1. A deductible – currently 20% of the prior year's direct earned premium on all lines of business covered in the TRIA program – up from 7% when the program first began.
2. Share of the losses above the deductible – the insurer still pays 15% of all losses above the deductible – up from 10%.
3. Industry aggregate retention – Federal government is required to recoup any losses from private industry up to $27.5 billion – up from $10 billion.

Further, an event must hit a certain "trigger level" in order for there to be any Federal involvement. The trigger is currently set at $100 million which is up from $5 million when the program was first started. Insurers are required to offer coverage for acts of terrorism on the same terms and conditions as other coverages, although this does not include coverage for NBCR attacks.

With the passage of TRIA, the fear that a worst-case terrorist event could render companies insolvent was somewhat reduced, making it possible these companies to continue to do business in higher-risk, urban areas. TRIA placed a ceiling on individual company terrorism losses, which permitted them to quantify their terrorism exposure and find a way to write the coverage.

TRIA IS NEEDED TO INCREASE PRIVATE INDUSTRY PARTICIPATION IN TERRORISM INSURANCE MARKET

In its 2010 report, the President's Working Group on Financial Markets concluded that the availability and affordability of terrorism risk insurance has improved over the last several years. The marketplace has increased capacity and prices have in general declined. However, the report also concluded that only about 60 percent of commercial insurance policyholders are buying terrorism coverage, a take-up rate that has remained flat for six years. Also, despite the fact that marketplace capacity has increased in general, it has remained very constrained in certain markets where policyholders have difficulty obtaining sufficient coverage.

Clearly private industry has at least a limited capacity to offer coverage for terrorism. However, we must recognize that the entire marketplace as it stands today has grown up in the presence of the TRIA program. We cannot hastily conclude that because the private sector can handle a portion of the risk, it could figure out a way to handle all of it. For one, capital is the key to availability, and insurance industry capital remains insufficient to absorb the cost of a large-scale terrorist attack. Further, capacity could disappear altogether for subsequent attacks. Simply put, the private sector's capacity is dwarfed for most modeled terrorism events and cannot be exposed beyond a reasonable level without failing in its primary purpose - supporting the economy by protecting against non-terrorism related losses and events. For example, in the case of workers compensation, in 2010 Marsh & McLennan have cited industry-wide capacity at only $30 billion, while the "worst case scenario" single loss is $90 billion.

Additional capital is needed in order to address this problem effectively. The private market is unable to absorb terrorism risk without a federal component. Even without a federal component, the government would bear the ultimate risk of uninsured losses as businesses and citizens turn to the federal government for assistance – the presence of a well-managed partnership program between the government and private insurers serves to ultimately *reduce*, not increase, federal liability for terrorism losses. The purpose of the partnership is not to protect insurers, but to make sure that the economy can recover in as orderly a fashion as possible from a terrorist event.

We would add that an effective public-private partnership also depends on participation by insurers of all sizes and structures. Any discussion of increasing private sector involvement in the TRIA program must be had with an eye toward ensuring participation by smaller and mid-sized insurers. Event trigger and deductible levels are key to the ability of these insurers to continue to provide coverage. Large increases in the trigger, company deductibles, or insurer co-payments could drive medium and small insurers out the market, reducing competition and further constraining availability of terrorism risk coverage. There have been no changes in the market that would change this calculus.

Difficulties in measuring risk, raising sufficient capital, and the limits on ability to constrain risk exposure, all point to the continuing need for a public-private partnership. Given that we cannot predict the severity or frequency of terrorist events, having a cap on what a company knows that it will have to pay allows it to at least begin to manage its risk exposures. Without a program, we would see a drastic reduction in both the availability and affordability of terrorism risk insurance like we did in the aftermath of 9/11.

CONCLUSION

It is much easier to argue the feasibility of a fully private market for terrorism insurance when no losses have been incurred since TRIA was enacted. Suffice it to say, the memory of the market immediately following 9/11 ought to give pause to anyone pushing to end the private/public partnership that has worked to provide commercial policyholders with the coverage they need. The result when the next terrorist attack occurs will be more − not less − federal exposure. In order to encourage private sector involvement in the terrorism insurance marketplace − and thereby protect and promote our nation's finances, security, and economic strength − we must maintain a long-term private/public partnership for terrorism risk insurance.

End Notes

[1] Insurance Information Institute, "Terrorism Risk: A Reemergent Threat." April, 2011, p. 15.
[2] Real Estate Roundtable, "Survey Confirms Economic Toll of Terrorism Insurance Gap: Over $10 Billion of Real Estate Projects Affected Across U.S.," September 4, 2002.
[3] President George W. Bush, "President Reiterates Need for Terrorism Insurance Agreement," October 3, 2002.

In: Terrorism Risk Insurance   ISBN: 978-1-62618-697-2
Editor: Oscar A. Madsen   © 2013 Nova Science Publishers, Inc.

Chapter 10

TESTIMONY OF MICHAEL LANZA, EXECUTIVE VICE PRESIDENT AND GENERAL COUNSEL, SELECTIVE INSURANCE GROUP, INC. HEARING ON "TRIA AT TEN YEARS: THE FUTURE OF THE TERRORISM RISK INSURANCE PROGRAM"[*]

Chairman Biggert, Ranking Member Gutierrez, Members of the Subcommittee:

Thank you for the opportunity to testify today on terrorism insurance issues. I am Michael Lanza, Executive Vice President and General Counsel of Selective Insurance Group, Inc. Selective is the 49th largest property and casualty insurance group in the country. I am testifying today on behalf of our national trade association, the Property Casualty Insurers Association of America (PCI), which represents approximately 40 percent of the nation's home, auto, and business insurance market.

Today we memorialize the anniversary of the tragic 9-11terrorist attack that killed thousands and resulted in economic devastation greater than any insured loss in history. With economic investment freezing, President Bush asked Congress to immediately enact legislation to protect our country's security. This Committee responded swiftly and passed the Terrorism

---

[*] This is an edited, reformatted and augmented version of a Testimony Presented September 11, 2012 before the House Committee on Financial Services, Subcommittee on Insurance, Housing and Community Opportunity.

Reinsurance Act, or TRIA, in just 2 months. In September 2002, the House adopted the TRIA conference report by voice vote. In 2005, and 2007, the House voted overwhelmingly to renew this important national security program. These three House votes passed by wide margins under different majorities – and reflect TRIA's historic bipartisan support.

In the last 11 years, the threat of terrorism has not receded. Dozens of terrorist attacks against our nation are attempted annually, with terrorists evolving new strategies to circumvent federal security. TRIA is a low-cost, fiscally prudent terrorism safety net that protects our nation's economic security. Absent its extension, insurance policies will begin in 2013 to exclude terrorism coverage or, to the extent permitted under state law, not be renewed for major underlying risks.

PCI and Selective strongly believe in the private insurance market. We also believe that the private insurance market can adequately cover risks that are fully insurable. Fully insurable risks are those for which a private insurer can adequately predict the likelihood and severity of a loss. We know terrorism when we see it, but it is difficult to define. Is it a crime or an act of war? Neither, however, is generally insurable – let alone fully insurable – in the private insurance market.

Some Committee Members who have philosophical concerns about government programs that support or displace private markets may have some philosophical doubts about TRIA. TRIA, however, is essential to the private insurance market because terrorism is not a fully insurable event. The likelihood and severity of terrorist attacks cannot be adequately predicted. Terrorism in the 9/11 form, which is what TRIA was designed to address, is an inherently unpredictable political act designed to frighten the nation's security and public through death, mutilation, and the destruction of public and private property. We know that after 9-11 the federal government set up costly victims' protection funds where private coverage was inadequate. TRIA has been the government's best security protection to keep the private sector largely responsible – and avoid future federal post-event bailouts.

National security is the primary responsibility of the federal government – not the private insurance market. Our national security apparatus is focused on anticipating and preventing terrorist acts and assessing the probability and severity of such events against major economic centers and public and private symbols of our country. These government agencies gather and have access to classified intelligence information not available to the private insurance market. Insurers analyze exposure to hypothetical terrorist events, but insurers don't have access to this sort of intelligence information necessary to predict the acts of terrorists. Our policyholders who purchase TRIA coverage (and in Selective's case that is 86% of our Commercial Lines policyholders and the mandated 100% of our workers compensation policyholders) also do not.

The pool of potential terrorists and the risk of terrorism are not static. They change based on U.S. domestic and foreign policy – which is constantly evolving. These policy changes, coupled with technological developments, can also lead to new forms of attack. The scope and breadth of these policy changes cannot be adequately predicted or tracked by the private insurance industry. Companies such as Selective, which writes primarily in 22 states east of the Mississippi and has approximately $1.6 billion in premium, certainly don't have the resources to do so. And Selective's small business clients, who pay an average of $10,000 for 3 commercial policies, certainly do not. This is why they need TRIA.

Let me elaborate on this. To be insurable, events must be predictable in frequency and severity. Property casualty insurers can estimate, based on experience, roughly how many car accidents, house fires, and industrial accidents will occur in a year and what their costs will be. With over a hundred years of weather history and free access to weather pattern science, the industry can also model storm paths and predict weather losses. This experience, and access to factual evidence and trends, however, does not exist for terrorism. In fact, only one data point exists for a catastrophic terrorist event – and that happened 11 years ago today.

Another difference between fully insurable events and terrorist acts is that insurable events are generally not correlated. That means they are random and independent of each other. For example, the likelihood of a hurricane in Florida is not correlated with the likelihood of an earthquake in California. The likelihood of correlated terrorist events is known and was demonstrated 11 years ago. Coordinated attacks can cause more terror, thus simultaneous attacks on New York City and Washington. Correlation of occurrence is another reason why we believe TRIA is required.

While *some* terrorism coverage is available in the private market now, it is not widely available for the reasons I have discussed – and because the potential losses are so large. Industry models have shown potential losses for another major terrorist event to be up to $250 billion. That figure is more than half the surplus for the entire property casualty insurance industry. Without TRIA, the private insurance market would have significant difficulty handling a loss of that magnitude.

There are three additional points about TRIA that I would like to make:

1. *TRIA Is Fiscally Responsible.* To date, TRIA has not cost taxpayers
    one cent in direct payments. If losses were to occur, the private
    insurance market would repay any government assistance up to $27.5
    billion. According to the CBO, TRIA's net cost to taxpayers through
    2017 is roughly zero. That's not bad for a program that helps ensure
    hundreds of billions of dollars in annual insurance coverage. In the
    absence of TRIA, taxpayers would face much more exposure. Without
    private insurance, the Federal government will step in to assist in a
    disaster. That means the demand for government assistance will be
    greater without the possibility of any TRIA recoupment.
2. *TRIA Protects Private Sector Growth.* The impetus behind TRIA was
    to prevent severe terrorism-related economic disruptions. Insurance is
    a substitute form of capital that supports balance sheets and permits
    businesses to own properties and engage in activities, such as hiring
    and business expansion, they might not otherwise do in its absence.
    Moreover, insurance permits immediate rebuilding after a loss.
    Without TRIA, insurers may simply exclude terrorism coverage or not
    renew policies covering major commercial risks to the extent
    permitted under state law. That means if there was a terrorist act, there
    would be less private capital to rebuild, which is key to the economy,
    economic development efforts, and public morale.
3. *TRIA Is Vital to Keeping the Cost of Workers Compensation Down.*
    State workers compensation laws mandate coverage for terrorist acts
    that occur in the workplace. Without TRIA, it will be very difficult to
    obtain reinsurance in the private market. This could lead insurers,
    where possible, to exit the workers compensation market. For those
    that remain in the market, the extent of losses could impair the ability
    to pay the claims of injured workers. Just as insurance is substitute
    capital for business, reinsurance is substitute capital for insurers.
    Without it, more capital would be required to support workers
    compensation writings. This would certainly drive up the costs of
    workers compensation insurance. This could be a significant
    impediment to economic recovery, particularly as it impacts small
    businesses.

Given what terrorism is, the private insurance markets cannot provide
terrorism coverage without TRIA. TRIA is a critical national security and
economic development program in which the private insurance market is

proud to participate. PCI stands ready to assist you as you continue your deliberations. Thank you very much.

In: Terrorism Risk Insurance
Editor: Oscar A. Madsen

ISBN: 978-1-62618-697-2
© 2013 Nova Science Publishers, Inc.

Chapter 11

TESTIMONY OF CHRISTOPHER M. LEWIS, SENIOR VICE PRESIDENT AND CHIEF INSURANCE RISK OFFICER, THE HARTFORD FINANCIAL SERVICES GROUP. HEARING ON "TRIA AT TEN YEARS: THE FUTURE OF THE TERRORISM RISK INSURANCE PROGRAM"*

Chairman Biggert, Ranking Member Gutierrez, and Members of the Subcommittee, thank you for the opportunity to appear before you today on behalf of The Hartford Financial Services Group (The Hartford) and our property-casualty insurance trade association, the American Insurance Association (AIA), to discuss the important issue of terrorism risk insurance. My name is Christopher Lewis and I am Senior Vice President and Chief Insurance Risk Officer for The Hartford. Founded over 200 years ago, The Hartford is one of our nation's oldest insurance companies, among the largest commercial property-casualty insurers, and an insurance partner to over one million small businesses across the United States.

In my capacity as a chief risk officer, I believe that I can offer an important perspective on why terrorism risk remains a unique and uninsurable risk, describe the limited tools available to insurers to manage that risk,

---

* This is an edited, reformatted and augmented version of a Testimony Presented September 11, 2012 before the House Committee on Financial Services, Subcommittee on Insurance, Housing and Community Opportunity.

explain the market stabilizing value of the program established by the Terrorism Risk Insurance Act of 2002 (TRIA) and its successors, and underscore the importance of maintaining this essential program into the foreseeable future to protect our economy in the event of another major terrorist attack on U.S. soil.

THE INSURANCE INDUSTRY'S RESPONSE TO SEPTEMBER 11, 2001

Today marks the 11th anniversary of the tragic attack on September 11, 2001. That event forced all Americans to confront directly the previously unforeseen realities associated with a catastrophic terrorist attack on U.S. soil – quite literally, to face a new form of war. Despite the unanticipated nature of the event, The Hartford and other insurers responded to September 11 claims in an unwavering manner and without a single dollar of federal assistance.

However, the devastating economic consequences of the attack forced insurers and other businesses to re-examine the nature of terrorism-related risks, as well as to review how such risks were being spread and managed.

In today's dollars, the September 11th attack is estimated to have resulted in almost 3,000 deaths, as well as over $23 billion in insured property loss and $40 billion in total insured loss1 The Hartford's share of this loss was approximately 3 to 3.5%, as we helped our policyholders recover from the tragic loss. Of course, a large portion of the insured industry loss was effectively reinsured, and the reinsurance industry honored its obligations.

Unfortunately, in the aftermath of the attack, the reinsurance markets withdrew new capacity and the reinsurance market for terrorism evaporated. Without the ability to spread and diversify these risks globally through reinsurance and with no ability to price the risk of terrorism, insurance companies were unable to provide adequate terrorism coverage to commercial policyholders. The effects of this chain of events trickled down to lenders and the construction industry, putting a significant drag on the economy. To support the economy and allow private markets to stabilize, Congress stepped forward in bipartisan collaboration and passed the Terrorism Risk Insurance Act of 2002 (TRIA).

TRIA provides a federal backstop to insurance companies for large certified terrorism events - above a $100 million loss - while requiring insurers to "make available" (offer) terrorism insurance to commercial policyholders for such coverage as business interruption and property insurance. Under the current program, insurers would need to absorb an estimated $25 to $30 billion of insured losses before the federal government begins to share the losses. Put another way, a terrorism loss would have to be larger than $25 to $30 billion before the federal government would be called on to make any payment. Even then, TRIA requires each insurer to pay 15 cents on every dollar of loss above its deductible, and then provides a recoupment mechanism to recover federal dollars that are expended.

By creating a post-event pooling mechanism that preserves significant industry "skin in the game" and only accesses federal dollars for extremely large-scale terrorism losses, the Act allows insurance companies to understand and manage their potential exposure to losses attributable to terrorism attacks while providing a cap on the potential loss to capital from such an attack. As a result, insurers are able to offer terrorism coverage to commercial policyholders while TRIA provides the all-important market stability.

In the event of a future terrorist attack, TRIA ensures that private insurance payments flow to those affected businesses that have purchased coverage, as well as to their employees, which in turn helps businesses and the economy recover. These payments will be crucial to minimizing the economic, psychological, and social fallout from an attack. At the same time, if an attack is so massive that it triggers the federal protection established by TRIA, government payments are ultimately recaptured through a recoupment mechanism that was established in the legislation. This greatly mitigates any costs of this federal program.

It is important to emphasize that taxpayers are protected at every step under TRIA. First, they benefit from the economic security that insurance coverage provides before an attack. Second, after an attack occurs, the immediate flow of claims payments provides stability and minimizes economic disruptions to those who suffer from the attack directly as well as to all Americans. And finally, in the event of a catastrophic terrorist attack that triggers the government program, any dispersed federal funds are ultimately repaid through TRIA's recoupment mechanism. Thus, TRIA is both a sensible and indispensable component of national economic security.

TERRORISM RISK IS A UNIQUE, UNINSURABLE RISK

A public-private solution is necessary for the risk of terrorism because, from an insurance perspective, terrorism does not meet the core characteristics of a privately "insurable peril." Private insurance markets are founded on the ability to (a) measure the likelihood and potential severity of loss to a policyholder for any specific peril and then (b) to effectively pool the loss experience across many policyholders exposed to relatively *homogeneous*, *random* and *independent* risks. Quite the opposite, terrorism involves an intentional act carried out at the direction of individual actors and groups with the explicit intention of maximizing overall loss of life, property, and economic disruption across as many insureds as feasible. Terrorists can pick the target, change the target at will to bypass security, and coordinate an attack on multiple targets in diverse locations. As result, terrorism, like war risks, fails the basic requirements for "ex ante" (before the event) pooling in the private insurance markets.

- Insurers lack any basis for assessing the likelihood or probability of a major terrorist attack, especially given the limited information that is publicly available. While insurers can price insurance when the nature of the risk is estimable but highly uncertain, ex ante insurance mechanisms fail when there is no credible basis for assessing the likelihood of an event.
- The potential magnitude or severity of large scale terrorist attacks, particularly those that involve the use of unconventional weapons involving nuclear, biological, chemical, and radiological (NBCR) agents, is largely unknown given the fortunate dearth of prior experience. While insurers can manage loss aggregations for "conventional" attack modes, the industry has limited information on managing exposures to wide-area loss event scenarios that would be the hallmark of NBCR attacks.
- Given the concentration of insured lives and property values in business centers, the risk of wide-area terrorism attacks poses a real solvency threat to insurers -- a threat that can easily eclipse that of natural disasters given the stated intention of a terrorist to exact maximal economic disruption.
- The interdependent nature of terrorism risks limits the markets' ability to rely on mitigation to manage exposures. Hardening a potential target may simply cause a terrorist to shift to a softer target or shift the manner of attack. Moreover, since a portion of a terrorist objective is to wage psychological war, the terrorist attacks can be directed throughout the U.S. – from New York City, to Chicago, to San Francisco and to the main streets of any town in between.

LIMITED RISK MANAGEMENT TOOLS ARE AVAILABLE

Even with the existence of TRIA, insurers' ability to manage terrorism risk is limited. From a coverage perspective, while TRIA requires a mandatory "offer" as a condition for participation, state laws actually mandate coverage for terrorism for certain lines of insurance. For example, in the 49 states that require workers' compensation insurance, on-the-job injuries are covered without exclusion, whatever the cause. Further, a number of states (including those with significant business centers) mandate that insurers cover terrorism-created fire losses, even if a policyholder does not purchase terrorism coverage. As a result, while an insurer may exclude NBCR terrorism coverage in some states, losses caused by the fire following an explosion from one of these perils would be covered.

Second, as noted above, the industry's lack of credible methods for assessing the likelihood of an attack limits our ability to determine an actuarially fair premium. As noted by the most recent report on terrorism risk insurance market conditions from the President's Working Group on Financial Markets (PWG Report), "despite the reported improvements in modeling to measure an insurer's aggregate loss exposure, the industry remains uncertain about the reliability of probabilistic models to predict frequency and severity of terrorist attacks."

Third, reinsurance capacity for terrorism losses is minimal. Citing many of the same issues identified above for primary insurance companies, reinsurance companies offer extremely limited capacity for terrorism risk and generally do not offer coverage for terrorist attacks committed with NBCR weapons. According to the PWG report, reinsurance capacity available for terrorism risk remains in the $6 billion to $10 billion range, an amount that is well below the estimated industry-wide retention figure under TRIA.

To provide some perspective, The Hartford's 2011 retention under the Terrorism Risk Insurance Program Reauthorization Act (TRIPRA) is approximately $1.1 billion in company losses. With respect to property, terrorism reinsurance of any material amount within this retention is effectively non-existent. In contrast, for natural catastrophe losses, The Hartford's principal corporate catastrophe treaty provides just under $700 million in reinsurance protection in excess of a $350 million deductible. The Hartford has an additional $400 million in reinsurance protection above $1.1 billion financed through non-traditional reinsurance markets (e.g., catastrophe bonds). As the person in the company responsible for purchasing reinsurance protection for The Hartford, I can attest that I wish that the reinsurance markets were willing to provide the same capacity for terrorism within our TRIA retention as is available for natural catastrophes. But the reinsurance capacity is simply not available. The recent PWG report is interesting in that it indicates that the total amount of reinsurance capacity is up slightly from prior studies. The small increase in reinsurance capacity, undoubtedly available to smaller companies, actually demonstrates the value of the TRIA program to "crowd in" additional reinsurance capacity – that is, it provides reinsurers some assurance that the reinsured companies can manage through a large scale event and remain viable trading partners after a loss.

Given these challenges, how do insurance companies manage the risk of terrorism today? The main tool available to manage the risk of terrorism is to limit exposure concentrations in potential "high target areas." If terrorism exposure concentrations get too high relative to surplus, an insurance company could non-renew entire commercial policies to reduce the terrorism exposure – often creating hardships for the underlying policyholders. These exposure concentrations are especially difficult for certain lines of business like workers' compensation and fire following coverage in certain states where exclusions for NBCR attacks are not recognized. Over the past 11 years, with the benefit of TRIA, the insurance industry has successfully managed these concentrations of exposure within the TRIA retentions. Policies shed by one company have generally been absorbed by a competitor.

Without TRIA, however, individual insurers would face large uncapped exposure and would face difficult choices about how to manage down exposures relative to capital, including facing decisions on whether or not to non-renew large portions of their commercial policyholder portfolios, especially given the fact that they cannot exclude the peril of terrorism from workers compensation coverage and fire following coverage in a number of states. For the record, we do not believe that this outcome would be in the best interests of our policyholders or the overall economy.

BOTTOM LINE: TRIA HAS WORKED

Almost ten years into TRIA, there should be no doubt that the program has brought stability to the private market and has enabled insurers to provide capacity despite the unique characteristics of terrorism risk. As the President's Working Group concluded at the end of 2010, "the Program provides incentive to property and casualty insurers and reinsurers who might not otherwise provide terrorism risk insurance at current capacity levels, or at current prices, absent Federal support or State law mandates. It does this by providing some degree of certainty of an insurers' maximum loss exposure." TRIA has been shown thus far to be a successful partnership among the federal government, insurers and policyholders to protect the economy in the event of an attack. Thanks to TRIA and its successors, The Hartford has been able to manage our terrorism exposure within acceptable limits while supporting our policyholders' need for terrorism coverage. In 2011, The Hartford's take-up rates for terrorism insurance were over 98%.

As a nation, we can take some comfort in the fact that since 9/11 and despite numerous attempts, terrorists have not succeeded in attacking U.S. interests on our soil. Other countries in the world have been less fortunate. The inescapable conclusion is that as long as this terrible risk threatens our way of life, we must fortify our economy against the potential consequences. TRIA and its successor programs have been very successful and continue to make terrorism coverage widely available. It is essential that the program is maintained so that the United States can enjoy national economic security for years to come.

End Note

[1] Source: Insurance Information Institute, 2010 dollars excluding Victims Compensation Fund.

INDEX

D

E

reserves, 69
resources, 27, 78, 95
response, 10, 20, 37, 47, 49, 59, 69, 82,
    86
restrictions, 24
retail, 65
retention rate, 75
revenue, 77
risk factors, 16
risk management, 63, 64, 65
risks, 3, 4, 8, 9, 21, 26, 27, 29, 31, 34, 48,
    49, 51, 52, 55, 56, 57, 58, 60, 64, 65,
    66, 67, 68, 73, 75, 78, 85, 87, 94, 96,
    100, 102
rural areas, 16

S

sadness, 59
safety, 65, 78, 94
scaling, 4
scarcity, 11
school, 66
science, 95
scope, 3, 79, 95
Secretary of the Treasury, viii, 2, 5, 6, 13,
    15, 16
securities, 77
security, 38, 64, 72, 74, 84, 85, 91, 93, 94,
    101, 102, 105
Senate, 4, 46, 60
September 11, vii, 1, 3, 4, 10, 11, 17, 18,
    19, 20, 21, 28, 31, 34, 35, 36, 39, 45,
    48, 49, 63, 71, 73, 77, 79, 83, 84, 93,
    99, 100
services, 37, 51, 60, 63, 77
settlements, 32
shareholders, 48, 56, 60, 66
shock, 21
showing, 11
signs, 11, 73
skin, 40, 101
small businesses, 63, 66, 96, 99

solution, 9, 42, 44, 68, 69, 75, 76, 101
Spain, 9, 25, 47, 54, 55
stability, 20, 21, 22, 24, 27, 31, 78, 84,
    101, 104
stabilization, 37
state, 3, 4, 6, 11, 18, 20, 39, 41, 50, 55,
    56, 94, 96, 103
state laws, 6, 103
state regulators, 3, 6
states, 3, 11, 21, 28, 49, 50, 65, 83, 88,
    95, 103, 104
storms, 55
stress, 38
structure, 31, 56, 75
substitutes, 26
suicide, 72
supply chain, 82
surcharges, viii, 2, 5, 11, 16, 43
surplus, 12, 95, 104
Switzerland, 25

T

tangible benefits, 31
target, 27, 43, 66, 82, 87, 102, 104
taxpayers, 28, 38, 40, 42, 43, 44, 47, 53,
    59, 74, 81, 96, 101
teams, 48
technological developments, 95
tenants, 65
tensions, 72
terrorism insurance, vii, 1, 6, 9, 10, 11,
    12, 19, 22, 24, 25, 28, 30, 36, 37, 39,
    41, 42, 43, 48, 49, 50, 51, 52, 58, 65,
    69, 72, 73, 74, 75, 76, 80, 81, 88, 91,
    93, 100, 105
Terrorism Insurance Program, vii, viii, 1,
    7, 68
Terrorism Risk Insurance Act of 2002
    (TRIA), vii, 49, 100
terrorist acts, 9, 11, 21, 27, 31, 48, 68, 88,
    94, 95, 96